A
PREACHER'S
COMPANION

Published by
The Bible Reading Fellowship
First Floor, Elsfield Hall
15–17 Elsfield Way, Oxford OX2 8FG

ISBN 1 84101 254 8
First published 2004
10 9 8 7 6 5 4 3 2 1 0
All rights reserved

Acknowledgments
Scripture quotations taken from The New Revised Standard Version of the Bible, Anglicized Edition, copyright © 1989, 1995 by the Division of Christian Education of the National Council of the Churches of Christ in the USA, are used by permission. All rights reserved.

Scripture quotations taken from The Revised Standard Version of the Bible, copyright © 1946, 1952, 1971 by the Division of Christian Education of the National Council of the Churches of Christ in the USA, are used by permission. All rights reserved.

Scripture quotations taken from the Holy Bible, New International Version, copyright © 1973, 1978, 1984 by International Bible Society, are used by permission of Hodder & Stoughton Limited. All rights reserved. 'NIV' is a registered trademark of International Bible Society. UK trademark number 1448790.

Extracts from the Authorized Version of the Bible (The King James Bible), the rights in which are vested in the Crown, are reproduced by permission of the Crown's patentee, Cambridge University Press.

Revised English Bible with the Apocrypha copyright © 1989 by Oxford University Press and Cambridge University Press.

p. 69: Extract from 'Dust' by Elizabeth Jennings, taken from Collected Poems, published by Carcanet, used by kind permission of David Higham Associates.
P. 69: Extract from Samuel Beckett's translation of an original by Miguel de Guavera, used by kind permission of John Calder Publishing.

A catalogue record for this book is available from the British Library

Printed and bound in Finland

A
PREACHER'S
COMPANION

ESSAYS FROM THE COLLEGE OF PREACHERS

EDITED BY

GEOFFREY HUNTER, GETHIN THOMAS
AND STEPHEN WRIGHT

In grateful memory of
Frederick Donald Coggan
1909–2000
Founder of the College of Preachers

LIST OF CONTRIBUTORS

Martyn Atkins is Director of Postgraduate Studies and Principal-Designate of Cliff College, Sheffield.

Richard Broadberry was formerly Vicar of St James, Riddlesdown, Purley.

Angela Butler is Priest-in-Charge of Hempsted and Diocesan Springboard Missioner for the Diocese of Gloucester.

Lavinia Byrne works in Somerset. She is a writer and a regular broadcaster with the BBC.

Douglas Cleverley Ford was Director of the College of Preachers from its inception in 1960 until 1973, and wrote many books concerned with preaching. He died in 1996.

Donald Coggan was the founder of the College of Preachers, and Archbishop of Canterbury from 1975 to 1980. He died in 2000.

Jane Craske is a tutor at Hartley Victoria Methodist College, Manchester.

David Day, formerly Principal of St John's College, Durham, is part-time curate of St Nicholas Church, Durham, and a writer.

Eric Devenport was formerly Bishop of Dunwich and, after his first retirement, Chaplain in Florence and Archdeacon of Italy and Malta.

David Dickinson is Methodist Minister in St Albans.

Peter Forster is Bishop of Chester.

Rod Garner is Vicar of Holy Trinity, Southport, and Theological Consultant in the Diocese of Liverpool.

Michael Henshall was formerly Bishop of Warrington and, from 1997 to 2003, Editor of *The Journal of the College of Preachers*. He is now Assistant Bishop in the Diocese of York.

Geoffrey Hunter was formerly Vicar of Heslington, York, and Chairman of the Executive Committee of the College of Preachers.

John James was Director of the College of Preachers from 1977 to 1985.

Paul Johns is a management consultant, broadcaster and Methodist local preacher.

James Jones is Bishop of Liverpool and was Chairman of the Council of the College of Preachers from 1999 to 2004.

Peter Kerr is Priest-in-Charge of Ombersley and Doverdale and Theological Adviser to the Bishop of Worcester.

Dwight Longenecker is a Catholic writer and broadcaster.

Jim McManus is Rector of the Redemptorist Centre of Spirituality at St Mary's, Kinoull, Perth.

Jolyon Mitchell is Senior Lecturer in the School of Divinity, Edinburgh University, and a former BBC World Service Producer.

Colin Morris is a Methodist minister, broadcaster and writer, and former Head of Religious Broadcasting at the BBC.

Lesslie Newbigin was Bishop in the Church of South India, Minister in the United Reformed Church and Moderator of its General Assembly 1977–78, and a teacher and writer. He died in 1998.

Barry Overend is Vicar of St Chad's, Far Headingley, Leeds, and a writer and broadcaster.

Ian Paton is Rector of Old St Paul's Church, Edinburgh, and Director of Liturgical Studies for the Theological Institute of the Scottish Episcopal Church.

Brian Pearson is Priest-in-Charge of Leek Wootton in the Diocese of Coventry, where he is also Director of Studies for Ordained Local Ministry.

Christine Pilkington is Principal Lecturer in Religious Studies, Canterbury Christ Church University College, and a Methodist local preacher.

Michael Quicke is Charles Koller Professor of Preaching and Communication at Northern Baptist Seminary, Chicago.

Susan Sayers is a writer of liturgical resources and an Anglican priest.

David Schlafer is a writer, editor, lecturer and independent consultant in preaching, based in Washington DC.

Leslie Stanbridge is Archdeacon Emeritus of York.

Roger Standing is Regional Minister/Team Leader with the Southern Counties Baptist Association.

Gethin Thomas is Training Programme Director at the School for Officer Training for the Salvation Army, William Booth College, London.

Michael Turnbull was formerly Bishop of Durham and Chairman of the Council of the College of Preachers.

Stephen Wright is Director of the College of Preachers and Associate Lecturer at Spurgeon's College, London.

CONTENTS

FOREWORD

This book is dedicated to the memory of Donald Coggan, Archbishop of Canterbury. He was a methodical and passionate preacher who founded the College of Preachers. He recognized the unique importance of proclamation in the life of the Church and its witness to the world. Even though I spent seven years of my life as an audio-visual producer and believe very much in the importance of modern media in communicating the Christian message, I stand with Donald Coggan in believing that preaching does have a unique role in the mission of God. There is no greater audio-visual than the human being. The sight and sound of a person captivated by the message they are proclaiming are compelling witnesses to the truth of the gospel.

One of Donald Coggan's important books is *The Sacrament of the Word* (SPCK), which is about the role of preaching. In the introduction he tells the story of an occasion when he is invited to dedicate a church that has been re-ordered. Before the service starts, he asks where he is to preach. They bring to him a contraption from which he says you would not deign to read even the notices for the week! After the service he berates the architect, asking for an understanding in our buildings that Anglicanism is bi-focal, with an equal emphasis on the word and the sacrament. The Archbishop asks the architect where the pulpit is. The architect replies by saying that he understands the Archbishop's concern and that he had raised this with the Vicar at the design stage. Apparently the Vicar had said there was no need for a pulpit because 'he preaches off the cuff'. This story is a parable of the demise of preaching in the Church today. Modern church architecture reveals the marginalizing of the word. No longer is it central to the worship of God.

Yet it has been estimated that a million sermons are preached every year in Britain alone. This important book ought to fall into the hands of as many of those preachers as possible! It has both theology and application. Preaching is both an art and a skill, and skills are something that can be acquired and improved by training. Here in these pages the preacher will find important guidance on how to improve technique. But technique alone is not sufficient. There needs to be a substantial theological grasp of what is at stake. You will find this substance also in these chapters.

The writers who grace these pages with their own insights are experienced preachers who have developed their own expertise over years of ministry. Taking to heart what is written here will ensure that preaching again comes centre stage in the Church.

One of the most important developments in the Church of England's new *Common Worship* confirmation service is the opportunity for the candidates to give their testimony. Unfortunately, in the past, preaching has often marginalized the laity and the telling of their story. People have concentrated too much on the professional minister as the only one who speaks when the Christian community gathers. This needs to be corrected. There needs to be much more opportunity in all our services for people to tell out how God has touched their life and inspired them to seek to do God's will on earth as it is done in heaven. The role of the preacher is to interpret these stories and to make connections between the experiences shared and the story that has been revealed by God through the Bible. When I take confirmation services I ask that the candidates have opportunity to tell their stories before I preach. It means that I have to think on my feet during the sermon, making connections between what I have just heard God's people say and what has been revealed in the Scriptures that I am expounding. It makes for adventurous preaching. It is a high-risk strategy! However, I never cease to thank God for the opportunity of being able to preach in this incarnational way. The raw material that comes from people's testimonies helps to earth the biblical message in the lives of the congregation.

There are many definitions of preaching but the one that I like the most is 'truth through personality'. That is certainly how it happened when Jesus preached. The preacher must be convinced by the message that he or she is communicating. As Donald Coggan writes in his opening paragraph about Paul the Preacher, 'The glory of being a herald of God took hold of him.' There is a divine imperative to preaching. All good preaching, too, ought to be a dialogue in that the preacher ought to be anticipating what the congregation might be thinking and asking in the light of the point being made. The good preacher is always anticipating so that the next point engages with exactly what the congregation wants to ask. A good preacher knows their congregation. They are aware of the pastoral situations in which their hearers live. They engage with them not just because of a particular style but because their preaching reveals a deep understanding of their hearers' situations.

I set myself a personal discipline of praying for four things each time that I preach. Firstly, I pray for power so that the word that goes forward through and from me might accomplish what God intends, namely that it brings life to the hearer. Secondly, I pray for love—a love for God in the moment of preaching and a love for the people. I am very aware that we can take into the pulpit all sorts of baggage of hurt, and use the sermon to settle scores or move agendas forward. May God save us all from such hectoring preaching. Instead, I pray for a love for God in the moment of proclamation so that that love, poured into our hearts by the Holy Spirit, might lead to a new and deeper affection for the people we are serving. Thirdly, I pray for authority, the sort of authority that characterized Jesus' teaching and preaching so that even when his detractors heard him they recognized that they had never head anybody speak with such authority. This authority is different from authoritarianism. It is the authority of someone who has been and is being shaped by the very Word that is being preached. Fourthly, I pray for truth, that through all the anecdotes, metaphors and parables people might see the Truth who is, of course, Jesus. I commend this prayerful approach to you.

In concluding my commendation of this book, let me address a question that is often asked by preachers: what is the difference between preaching and teaching? The answer, I think, is that although much preaching involves teaching, the difference is that after teaching, discussion is entirely appropriate, whereas after preaching, discussion is entirely inappropriate. Teaching leads to analysis, discussion, questions about application. Preaching is, in the end, an appeal to the will. I often come away from a service with this simple question in my heart and mind: 'Lord, did you speak?'

When I was serving in a parish, we would give out sermon assessment forms to members of the congregation from time to time. This, as you will appreciate, was a nerve-racking experience! When the returns came in, however, they were always instructive and helpful in developing preaching. I would encourage you to engage in such an exercise and to set your own questions from these chapters to see how you might improve your own ability as a preacher. The fifth part of this book gives very important practical suggestions that will provide the reader with a valuable resource. Once you have read the book, keep it to hand!

The Rt Revd James Jones, the Bishop of Liverpool

INTRODUCTION

This volume is offered as a resource for preachers. Through a series of short articles, mostly between 500 and 2000 words in length, it seeks to stimulate reflection and provide an anchor-point for practice across a range of aspects of preaching.

Many of the articles are edited versions of material that has appeared over the years in *The Journal of the College of Preachers* (formerly known as *The Fellowship Paper*). (Such articles are indicated by a date following the title; those with no date have been newly commissioned.) The College was founded in 1960 by a small group of Anglicans concerned about the quality of preaching in the Church of England. The group included some prominent figures such as Bryan Green, Frank Lake, Geoffrey Lampe, C.F.D. Moule, George Reindorp and Max Warren. The founding Chairman of the College, to whose memory this book is gratefully dedicated and to whom tribute is paid on the following pages, was Donald Coggan, then Bishop of Bradford, subsequently Archbishop of York and Archbishop of Canterbury.

Over the years, the College has offered an increasing number and range of training courses, and a journal which has likewise grown in size and reach. For many years, the Fellowship Paper consisted largely of sermon outlines, mostly written by the College's first Director, Douglas Cleverley Ford. Gradually a wider range of contributors was involved. In recent years, the sermon outlines have been supplemented by substantial articles on various aspects of preaching, as well as book reviews. Many of the articles, including some of those reproduced here, were versions of presentations which had been given at College courses and conferences.

Two points are worth making concerning the focus and ethos of the present collection and the items of which it is composed.

First, we have aimed that this should be an ecumenical collection—that is, that it should be of interest and service to preachers in all the mainstream Christian denominations and traditions. Since the 1980s, the College has steadily branched out from its Anglican roots, so that now at all levels of its structures and activities there is a rich mixture of Christians from different backgrounds.

The ecumenical nature of the volume means that readers should not expect to find unanimity of perspective here. Genuine differences of standpoint among Christians do, of course, show themselves when it comes to preaching, as in other aspects of church life. Yet it is interesting also to observe the extent to which preaching can be a focus of unity. Those with a deep commitment to preaching, such as the contributors to this book, often find themselves drawn together despite considerable differences of outlook on many things, even on methods of preaching! No doubt this is because, at root, the commitment to preach stems from the Jesus they long to share—and he is the same Christ for all. This book makes no attempt to resolve differences that appear, but by juxtaposing various angles we hope that it may prompt readers to a deeper consideration of the basis and nature of Christian preaching.

Second, we have designed this as a practical collection. The College has always been concerned first and foremost with the needs of the regular preacher for encouragement, stimulus and resources. This has never entailed a simplistic approach, and the College has always encouraged wrestling with the thinkers who shape the many disciplines that touch upon preaching—notably theology, biblical studies, cultural studies and communication studies. In the early publications it is interesting to note the engagement with the continental ideas of Barth and Bultmann; more recently, it is more likely to be transatlantic names such as Buttrick and Brueggemann that crop up. Although it now offers, in partnership with Spurgeon's College, London, courses in preaching validated by the University of Wales, the College continues to serve a wide constituency beyond those in a position to undertake academic courses.

So this is not an academic book on preaching. There is a growing specialist literature on homiletics as a discipline in its own right (though it is still more voluminous in North America than in the United Kingdom) and there are many places to turn for further exploration of the subjects opened up in these short articles. Nor does it aim to be anything like encyclopedic in scope: the history of preaching, for instance, is largely excluded. Readers seeking an encyclopedia of preaching are referred to that edited by William Willimon and Richard Lischer (Westminster John Knox Press, 1995).

This book seeks, then, to be a companion on the way for the preacher who may be sometimes excited, sometimes daunted by the task, but who is always in need of support. Some may be drawn to one section rather than another; we hope that all will enjoy 'dipping'.

We are grateful to all the contributors to this volume (a few of whom are now departed). I am personally grateful to Spurgeon's College, London, which has provided a most congenial base of operations for me for the past five years; and to the executive committee of the College of Preachers, especially its chairman, the Right Reverend James Jones, and vice chairman, the Reverend Peter Barber, for their support for this project and for me as the College's Director. Special thanks are due to the two members of the Committee, Canon Geoffrey Hunter and Major Gethin Thomas, who have shared in the editorial task, not least by sifting through 40 years' worth of journals.

Any project like this depends on a range of people, and I want to pay special tribute to those who have assisted with correspondence and with copying and scanning old documents: Karen Atkin of the College of Preachers, Sandra Atkinson and Joy Gadsden of Spurgeon's College, and Cath Blackwell of William Booth College. Their support has been willing and vital.

It is very good that the College has been able to work on this book with the Bible Reading Fellowship, and I am particularly thankful to the Commissioning Editor, Naomi Starkey, for her encouragement and patience. Both organizations owe a huge debt to Donald Coggan and we trust that this book will be a small but worthy tribute to him.

Stephen Wright

⁊

FREDERICK DONALD COGGAN,
1909–2000

Michael Turnbull (2001)

It is no exaggeration to say that without Donald Coggan the British College of Preachers would not have begun. Inspired by his visits to the College of Preachers in Washington, he saw the need for something along similar lines in the UK. He personally raised the money for its foundation, appointed its first director, gave it permanent status, and took a very active part in the content of its courses and the style of its operation. It was Donald Coggan who saw that the British college should have one major difference from that in America—it would not be based on a residential building but capture the spirit of many great preachers by being itinerant. In this way the courses that the college offered became available to many more preachers.

Right up to the last years of his life and well into his eighties Donald Coggan would appear at Council meetings and travel great distances to speak at college occasions and conferences. The great offices he held— Bishop of Bradford, Archbishop of York, Archbishop of Canterbury— never overwhelmed him to the extent that he neglected the College of Preachers. There is no doubt that the college was one of the loves of his life. That was not because he liked organizations—he once referred to another piece of church machinery as 'institutionalized fog'. He worked to keep the College of Preachers on the road because of a number of deeply held convictions.

In the first place Donald Coggan's understanding of God was of one who speaks, in creation, in the redeeming One and in the communicating power of the Holy Spirit. In the many-layered meanings of the Trinity, there was to be found a dynamic which was the Word. If we are close to God, and Donald Coggan was a man of disciplined and profound prayer, then we shall be infected by his Word. Donald Coggan said that God was the one who spoke because he loved, and he drew comparisons with human love. Because we love we can do no other but speak, however inadequate our words seem to be.

This was, for Donald Coggan, the imperative of preaching. It was not in the first place to impress or change his hearers; it was because he could do no other. It was inextricably part of his discipleship. The love of Christ impelled him to speak—that was the heart of Donald Coggan's understanding of preaching. Quite a long way from being a technical chore!

Out of this sprang a high doctrine of preaching which Donald Coggan longed to see in every part of church life. He wanted prayer book, furniture and liturgy to express the distinctive Anglican balance of word and sacrament. He demanded that the theology of preaching and its practice was thoroughly taught to ordinands and Readers. He was scathing of reordered churches that failed to demonstrate the place of the word alongside the sacrament. As Bishop and Archbishop, Donald Coggan would exemplify this in his own preaching. At confirmations and especially at institutions of new clergy, where he knew there would be a number of clergy and Readers present, he would take great pains to open up a single word from the Greek New Testament and apply it in arresting fashion to the needs of the parish.

Linked with this high doctrine was his fervour for evangelism. From his student days among the beach missions of CSSM, to his worldwide mission as Archbishop, he seldom missed an opportunity to demonstrate the gospel and to look for conversion. But he also knew that growth was as important as birth—growth towards God, growth in understanding, growth in love. His teaching was never simplistic but always accessible, often marked, like his writing, with brief staccato sentences which embedded themselves on the mind of his hearers.

Donald Coggan's prolific writing about preaching included a ready sympathy for preachers. He recognized the particular discipline of preaching to the same people week after week, of giving time to preparation among so many other demands and of making the sermon relevant without being merely topical. But at the same time he had a great sympathy for those who listen to sermons, recognizing that many who come thirsting are often given only a dry sponge. So he worked to encourage preacher and congregation to come together to learn of each other's needs.

The best way of discovering Donald Coggan's view of preaching is to read his books. They are a fine legacy. Many were written in recent times, but his early work still speaks to today's condition. *Convictions* (1975) is a compilation of addresses and sermons, mostly from his time at York. His books specifically on preaching include *The Ministry of the Word* (1945), *Stewards of Grace* (1958), *Word and World* (1971), *On Preaching* (1978), *The Sacrament of the Word* (1987, revised as *A New Day for Preaching*, 1996). He wrote other books which are useful for preachers: *Five Makers of the New Testament* (1962), *Prayers of the New Testament* (1967), *Paul—Portrait of a Revolutionary* (1984), *Meet Paul: An Encounter with the Apostle* (1997), and his recently published *People's Bible Commentary* on the Psalms (in two volumes, 1998 and 1999). All should be on a preacher's bookshelf.

This is not the place for a full obituary of a great man of the 20th-century church, but the College of Preachers salutes him for the teaching and inspiration which continues into a new century. Our founder, above all, was a man of God who bore, sometimes painfully, God's love for humankind. His scholarship was combined with humanity. His gravitas was threaded with humour. His leadership was tempered with compassion. His very life was his finest sermon.

INTRODUCTION

Stephen Wright

What are the models available to us as preachers? With what basic understanding of our task do we work? There are many possible models, and most are by no means mutually exclusive. In this part of the book we present six.

The obvious starting-point for models of preaching is the Bible. Here we find a rich array. We could look to the prophets of the Old Testament. We could look to Jesus himself (and reference is made to his methods in Part 3). But perhaps the model to which we can approximate most closely, given that we are in the same position of 'bearing witness' to Jesus (Acts 26:16), is Paul. It is entirely appropriate that this collection should start with a study of the message and manner of Paul, and that it should come from Donald Coggan.

As the events of the first Good Friday and Easter have become more remote in time, Christians have needed to reflect on the meaning of our continuing proclamation of the gospel. Simply to imitate Paul (or another biblical figure) as a preacher is not enough, for we are in a different historical situation. Jim McManus offers us a theology of preaching that holds together the importance of witness to the historical *kerygma*—Paul's gospel—with the need to interpret the present time and the reality that God continues to speak afresh through (even despite) his servants.

Two ways of understanding the dynamics of preaching, sometimes in tension yet both surely vital, are presented in the next two articles. On the one hand, preaching is at the centre of the great outgoing missionary thrust of the church. Michael Quicke threads together two inseparable implications of this: preaching is evangelism, sharing good news; and preaching is bound up with the embodiment of God's kingdom in Christian service. On the other hand, as Peter Forster shows, preaching is a sacrament, a moment of encounter and promise when God's people are gathered in worship. The two approaches are one in their stress on preaching as an event, not mere words, and as equipment of the saints for following Jesus into the world.

The last two models look at aspects of the human dimension of preaching—a dimension which, we should not forget, God chooses to use, but which can easily be overlooked in more theological treatments. David Schlafer explores the notion of preaching as 'sacred play', suggesting something of the excitement of preaching when we let our God-given creative powers get to work with it. Colin Morris compares the preacher to others who 'perform' in public. The sense of difference between a preacher's calling and that of (say) an actor should not cause us to overlook the challenges common to both, nor the skills both are called to develop.

∞

PAUL THE PREACHER

Donald Coggan (1990)

The Times' obituary notice (10 July 1990) of the great Scottish preacher James Stewart described him thus: 'This shy, small man became almost incandescent once in a pulpit when the glory of being a herald of God took hold of him.' I imagine it was like that with Paul.

I imagine. Have we anything more than imagination to go on? We have, but not as much as we should like. If only we had some recordings, some tapes of the apostle at work in Corinth or Ephesus or Athens! If only there had been television cameras at work to fill out Luke's tantalizingly slender description.

For the rest we are dependent on Paul's own letters, from which we learn more about content than about manner of delivery; and that is as it should be, for technique, important as it is, ranks second to content—always.

Apart from speeches made in his own defence (Acts 20:18ff.; 22:1ff.; 24:10ff.; 26:2ff.), which cannot be regarded as examples of his *preaching*, Luke gives us only two sermons and they, presumably, are only intended to be resumés.

THE CONTENT OF PAUL'S PREACHING

In the first, Luke depicts Paul giving an address in the synagogue at Pisidian Antioch (Acts 13:16–41). He addresses his Jewish 'brothers... and others among you who worship God' (v. 26), that is godly Gentiles who felt drawn to the monotheistic Jewish religion. He begins with a brief reference to God's dealings with his people from the days of their fore-fathers to the time of John the Baptist. Then he comes straight to the crucifixion and resurrection of Jesus which he sees as a fulfilment of Scripture. He ends with a reference to forgiveness and faith and a warning about the judgment which awaits those who scoff at God's action. Paul and Barnabas were asked to return on the following Sabbath. They did so, only to find rejection on the part of the Jews. They turned to the Gentiles.

The sermon that Paul gave at Athens (Acts 17:22–31) has often been regarded as a failure. Those who hold that view say that it smacks of worldly wisdom—he quotes from pagan authors, it was not very successful, and when he went on to Corinth he changed not only the style but the content, determined as he was to preach Christ and him crucified (1 Corinthians 2:2).

I do not hold that view. Paul began by establishing a base of belief that he and his hearers shared—a creator Lord of heaven and earth who 'does not live in shrines made by human hands' (disillusionment with polytheism was rife among the intellectuals of the first century AD). Quoting authors known to many listening to him, he spoke of a God in 'whom we live and move, in him we exist', a God whose 'offspring' he and they were. From that common base, he launched out into themes of repentance, of world judgment, and of a man destined to judge, a man raised from the dead. Indeed, Luke specifically makes a point that Paul, though initially misunderstood, 'was preaching about Jesus and the Resurrection' (v. 18). And there were results—some negative, others positive, the latter including 'a member of the Council of the Areopagus, and a woman named Damaris, with others beside' (v. 34).

The approach at Antioch differs from that at Athens. But both sermons come home, unmistakably, to the crucified and risen Christ.

THE MANNER OF PAUL'S PREACHING

What did his opponents mean when they said that, in contrast to his 'weighty and powerful' letters, Paul himself was 'unimpressive, and as a speaker he is beneath contempt' (2 Corinthians 10:10)? It was frank of Paul to report this! Perhaps their remarks tell us more about them than they do about the apostle. Were they referring to a body battered by travel and persecution, and a delivery marked more by passion than by polish? Had his message been just that bit too near the bone to be pleasant? 'Beware when all speak well of you...'

What did he himself mean when he said that he came to the Corinthians 'without any pretensions to eloquence or wisdom in declaring the truth about God' (1 Corinthians 2:1)? Was he afraid of tickling their ears rather than piercing their consciences? And why did he come before them 'in weakness and fear, in great trepidation' (1 Corinthians 2:3)? He was not afraid of them—of that we can be sure. He was afraid of so handling the many-splendoured thing that he marred its glory. Can we not detect an element of awed surprise in this—'to me, who am less than the least of all God's people, he has granted the privilege of proclaiming to the Gentiles the good news of the unfathomable riches of Christ' (Ephesians 3:8), and is it not the death of preaching when that element is missing?

'Woe is me if I preach not the gospel'—that is the AV rendering of 1 Corinthians 9:16. The REB goes further: 'It would be agony for me not to preach', and that translation puts its finger on the secret that turned Paul's preaching from being a tyranny into being a passion.

THE PASSION OF PAUL'S PREACHING

Why this passion? What was it that drove Paul from Tarsus to Rome, with a longing (was it ever fulfilled?) to reach Spain, the very limits of the world? Why must he preach in places where the gospel had never come, pushing out the frontiers of his mission? Why be so careless about his own safety, heedless of his own comfort?

It was not that he had a new philosophy to teach, nor, primarily, a new ethic to expound. It was an event, a unique event which was itself a Person. It was an intrusion of God, an invasion from above, which centred in the life, death, and resurrection of a Man who was more than a man, one who stood with us and died for us even 'when we were yet sinners' (Romans 5:8). The Christ-event is absolutely central to all the preaching of Paul. Without that event, it would fall to pieces.

This is evidenced by the language Paul used when he was describing his life-work. His preaching was an 'announcement of good news', a 'publishing' of Christ, a 'heralding' of 'Christ Jesus as Lord, and ourselves as your servants for Jesus' sake' (2 Corinthians 4:5). He saw himself as an 'ambassador', representing his Sovereign in a foreign culture, speaking not of himself, or as a private person, but for his King and in his King's name (2 Corinthians 5:20).

THE DIMENSIONS OF PAUL'S PREACHING

Here was a man deeply concerned with everyday mundane matters—morals, money, marriage, the building of church units, the fashioning of character, the relationships that are the warp and woof of everyday living. But here was also a man who dealt in terms of eternity. If he was concerned with this life—and he undoubtedly was—he was also concerned with death and with the life to come. He treated death with the seriousness it deserved: after all, we all have to face it. 'Death is nothing at all,' said Henry Scott Holland. Paul would have said nothing so facile. Death is humanity's last enemy—but it is a conquered enemy. That was his message.

Paul stretches us. He keeps the tension between the temporal and the eternal, and in that very tension finds the virility of his message. He elaborates the contrasts between the shortlived troubles and the eternal glory, the things that are seen and the things that are unseen, the earthly frame and the God-provided building, the temporal home in the body and the eternal home with the Lord (2 Corinthians 4:16—5:10). Rob Paul of his eschatological and apocalyptic element and you rob him of the thrust of his gospel. All right: he was wrong in thinking that the great Day of the Lord was just around the corner. But was he wrong in speaking of a 'tribunal' before which all of us will stand and of a day when 'the universe itself is to be freed from the shackles of mortality and is to enter upon the glorious liberty of the children of God' (Romans 8:21)? I think not.

THE RELEVANCE OF PAUL'S PREACHING

This is not a matter of dry academic interest. It has to do with the thrust of our regular preaching ministry. There was a time when critics complained, with some justification, that Christians were so heavenly minded that they were no earthly use—their creed was lamentably weak in its application of belief to ethics. Has the pendulum now swung too far in the opposite direction? When we soft-pedal the eternal, men and women vote with their feet and with heavy hearts leave the church to seek elsewhere some answers to the problems of sin and suffering, of death and the life to come, of salvation (in the vast meaning that that concept holds in the pages of Scripture and especially in the teaching and preaching of Paul).

We may note that balance which Paul maintains in his letters (and so we assume he maintained in his preaching) between the *individual* and the *corporate* aspects of the Christian faith.

No one could state with greater clarity than Paul the intimacy of his personal relationship with his Lord. 'The Son of God loved me and gave himself up for me' (Galatians 2:20). 'For to me life is Christ…' (Philippians 1:21). He could never forget the encounter on the Damascus road nor the commission that followed it. Life from that time on was one long aspiration 'to take hold of that for which Christ once took hold of me' (Philippians 3:12). There can be nothing closer than that.

But the corporate aspect of his discipleship and of his faith is equally clear. The church as the Body of Christ with its constituent members, the church as the building growing up into a holy temple, a common baptism into Christ's death and a resurrection into his new life—these are dominant and powerful concepts in his thinking. Indeed, it is in the holding together, in the tension of the individual and the corporate, that the power of his message comes through.

Is the church waiting—is the revival of our preaching waiting—for an invasion of preachers, men and women, who dare to wrestle anew with the preaching of Paul, apostle and slave of Jesus Christ, and to let him invade their pulpits?

A THEOLOGY OF PREACHING

Jim McManus (1993)

A parish priest had to work late on Saturday night to get his homily ready for Sunday. In the morning he mounted the pulpit and began with the sign of the cross, 'In the name of the Father, the Son and the Holy Spirit'.

He looked down on his congregation. There, sitting right in front of his pulpit, was Monsignor Ronald Knox, the learned translator of the Bible, and the best-known Catholic preacher of his time. He paused, drew a deep breath and said, 'In the name of the Father, the Son and the Holy Spirit,' and left the pulpit!

That priest probably felt he had nothing very bright to say to Ronald Knox. In his moment of panic he forgot that God might have had something very important to say to Knox, and that God needed his voice to say it.

Preaching is a mystery. It is not simply an exercise of human discourse. Preaching is the proclamation of the word of God in and through human discourse. In and through the word of the preacher, the word of God is spoken to the community and to the individual. And through hearing the word of God the community is called to faith and conversion.

INCARNATION

Preaching can only be understood in the light of the mystery of the Incarnation. Just as the eternal Word of God, in order to become truly human and speak with a human voice, became incarnate and concealed his divinity, so Christ, in our time, in order to proclaim his gospel in our age, conceals his voice and his word in the voice and word of his preacher.

The Word of God is definitively revealed in Christ. There can be no true preaching if Christ is not being proclaimed. Archbishop Ramsey said, 'Jesus Christ came not only to preach a gospel but to be a gospel.' The purpose of the proclamation of Christ is not to impart information about Christ, but to make Christ, who is the gospel, present to those who hear the gospel.

Christian preaching, then, must always be the proclamation of the gospel of Christ, not in the words and images of the first century, but in the words and images that the men and women of our time can understand. The first-century preachers grappled with their faith in the mystery of Jesus and proclaimed that faith to their communities: we grapple with our faith in the mystery of Jesus and proclaim our faith to our communities. But the norm of our faith, like the norm of the first preachers of the gospel, is the *kerygma*, the gospel, the 'good news', the teaching, the life, the promises, the Kingdom and the mystery of Jesus Christ, the Son of God, as that mystery is normatively enshrined in the holy Scriptures and in the tradition of the church.

KERYGMA

The preacher is not a philosopher, offering reflections on the state of the world. He is a servant of the Word, proclaiming God's great love for the world.

The *kerygma* does not remain in the text, nor simply on the lips of the preacher. The *kerygma* penetrates the mind and the heart of the hearer and produces the response, 'You are the Christ, the Son of the living God.' The preaching of the *kerygma*, the saving death and resurrection of Jesus, evokes this response of personal faith, because it is Christ himself who is speaking. Each person must come to this personal faith, where profession of faith is not based simply on what others say, but on one's own inner conviction. Christ himself attributes this profession of faith to this work of the Father: 'Flesh and blood did not reveal this to you, but my Father who is in heaven' (Matthew 16:17). Preaching is the means through which we are offered the gift of this personal faith.

PREACHING AS A PRIMARY DUTY

It has often been said that Catholics are over-sacramentalized and under-evangelized. The reason for this can be found in the Catholic over-reaction to the Protestant Reformation.

While the Reformers emphasized the word of God, Catholics emphasized the sacraments, and for a few centuries we lost sight of the fact that the sacraments themselves 'draw their origin and nourishment from the word of God'. The neglect of the word of God in the celebration of the sacraments led to a downgrading of the sermon during Mass. The sermon was not considered part of the act of worship; indeed it was often viewed as an intrusion into the act of worship.

This defence of 'the Catholic Church of the Sacraments' against 'the Protestant Church of the Word' was officially ended at Vatican II. The act of worship consists of both word and sacrament and the fruitful celebration of the sacrament presupposes the proclamation of the word. Far from being an intrusion into the act of worship, the homily during the Mass is 'to be highly esteemed as part of the liturgy itself' (*Constitution on Liturgy*, paragraph 52). The Vatican Council clearly teaches that the primary duty of the priest is to preach the gospel.

Priests are still trying to come to terms with this perspective of the Vatican Council. Not only is preaching presented as their primary duty, but their homily during Mass is now considered part of the very worship that the community offers to God! As a result of this new perspective, preaching is being renewed.

'PRESENT TENSE' PREACHING

The living Word of God interprets the present situation for us, not in the past tense, but in the present tense. The preacher doesn't just tell us what God did in the past. That is sacred history. The preacher proclaims what God is doing now. That is news. That is why we call the message we have to deliver 'good news' or gospel.

Albert Nolan writes, 'There is a definite shape, certain characteristics, that any message would have to have in order to qualify as a true gospel, as a gospel of Jesus Christ for a particular people at a particular time. The first and most general of these characteristics is the message must be good news' (*God in South Africa*, Eerdmans, p. 8).

Nolan concludes that the greatest temptation for the preacher is 'to preach a timeless gospel of timeless truths that are equally applicable to all times and in all circumstances. Whatever value this might have it is simply not the gospel; it does not have the shape of news, let alone good news; it has the shape of doctrine, dogmas, principles, norms and eternal truths' (p. 15).

The preacher is not a lecturer, imparting more information about God; the preacher is a prophet, proclaiming 'good news from God'. The preacher helps the community to see God at work in daily life. The God whom the community gathers to worship is not a distant God. His name is Emmanuel and he is to be found in every human situation, at the heart of every human experience. The task of the preacher is to enable the community to hear this liberating but challenging word. The gospel message is not just for the spiritual dimension. It is for the human community in its total environment.

PRAYERFUL PREACHING

'Universalizing' the message, turning 'news' into doctrine, may be the greatest temptation of the preacher. The second greatest temptation surely is not taking the time necessary for prayer and reflection in order to hear the word oneself and so be more open to proclaim it. The modern church is even more complicated than the early church. All the more reason, then, for the preachers of the word to say, 'But we will give ourselves continually to prayer and the ministry of the word' (Acts 6:4).

No other good work should take the preacher away from the primary duty to pray, hear and proclaim the word. Archbishop Coggan quotes the warning of Dr Vance Havner: 'I think preachers are getting lost in a multitude of smaller duties. The preacher has a peculiar place in the economy of God. He is in danger of becoming so involved with secondary affairs that he loses his prophetic gift. The devil doesn't care how great a success a preacher is in any field, if he can just kill the prophet in him' (D. Coggan, On Preaching, SPCK, p. 13).

If faith comes through preaching, we must hold with great conviction that the renewal of faith in our time depends, in no small measure, on the liberation of the preacher to preach.

⚮

PREACHING AS A
MISSIONARY ACTIVITY

Michael Quicke (1999)

Many people, inside the church as well as outside, view preaching and
mission as though they are at odds. They see preaching as a luxury diet
for the committed few. It occurs within church buildings; it assumes the
Bible is relevant and that people will be willing to sit still for 10 to 20
minutes—in exceptional circumstances even more. But with 74,700
sermons preached every week in the UK, and church numbers declining
massively over the last two decades, many argue that this just proves how
ineffective preaching is in mission.

I believe this distinction is grossly overstated and has opened up an
unhealthy gap between preaching and mission. They belong together and
they need each other. The mission of preaching is the mission of God.
The preaching of mission is the mission of God.

In recent times a great variety of theologians, Protestant and Catholic,
have embraced the idea of the 'mission of God'. Mission is no less than
God's activity in the world to transform it through the sending of Jesus
Christ and the establishment of his kingdom.

The Manila Manifesto of 1989 (Lausanne Committee for World
Evangelization, Pasadena) calls 'the whole church to take the whole gospel
to the whole world' (p. 7). Note also its important comment: 'Evangelism
is primary because our chief concern is with the gospel, that all people
may have the opportunity to accept Jesus Christ as Lord. Yet Jesus not
only proclaimed the Kingdom of God. He also demonstrated its arrival by
works of mercy and power. We are called today to a similar integration of
words and deeds' (p. 15).

Luke 4:18–19 is a paradigmatic text for mission and preaching. Here
Jesus heralds an upside-down kingdom where all the things the world
admires and seeks are brought tumbling down.

G.A. Buttrick wrote: '[I]t is a fair presumption that Jesus could have written books. Instead, "Jesus came preaching". He trusted his most precious sayings to the blemished reputation and the precarious memory of his friends... Of a truth it is a printed New Testament that remains, but its vital power is drawn from a word and a Person... The gospel was and is a living impact' (*Jesus Came Preaching: Christian Preaching in the New Age*, Charles Scribner's, pp. 17f.).

At the birth of the church, with the accompanying fireworks of the Spirit, it was by Peter's preaching that the gospel was heard and responses were made (Acts 2:36–38). As the mission of the early church moved pulsatingly outwards, the apostle Paul emerged on the front-line as he gave everything he had to the preaching task. He provided a memorable summary of its extraordinary power: 'God was pleased through the foolishness of what was preached to save those who believe' (1 Corinthians 1:21). He spells out the necessity of preaching in the chain reaction of faith: 'How, then, can they call on the one they have not believed in? And how can they believe in the one of whom they have not heard? And how can they hear without someone preaching to them? And how can they preach unless they are sent? As it is written: "How beautiful are the feet of those who bring good news"' (Romans 10:14–15). Notice the quotation from all-action Isaiah 52:7, and how this injects further dynamic into the preaching event. Preaching is not only about a voice being heard: it is also about feet moving. The preacher has to go to the right place at the right time.

How is it then that there is sometimes a perception that God's mission is better carried on by means other than preaching?

One reason is *fear*. Craig Loscalzo suggests that we may shy away from proclaiming the message because we fear we lack expertise, because we fear failure, and because we fear offending people (*Evangelistic Preaching that Connects: Guidance in Shaping Fresh and Appealing Sermons*, IVP, pp. 32–35). He says that 'fears will subside when we recognize the content of our message... is good news... Good news is easy to share, open-mindedly and respectfully' (p. 35).

The theme of boldness threads right through the New Testament and church history. When Timothy is exhorted to 'preach the word' (2 Timothy 4:2) we are probably closer to what we understand as a continuous preaching ministry within the church than anywhere else in Scripture: 'Be prepared in season and out of season; correct, rebuke and encourage—with great patience and careful instruction.' This does not sound an easy task. Earlier in the letter there is the specific challenge: 'For God did not give us a spirit of timidity but a spirit of power, of love and of self-discipline' (2 Timothy 1:7).

Many of us have deep fears about offending people. There is too often a guilty silence when it comes to 'preaching to the will' (as Sangster put it). Boldness was essential when the apostles first preached because of the atmosphere of hostility and persecution. They were preaching Christ and the resurrection to people who did not want to hear. I sense hostility today against the same claims.

The preacher has an awesome responsibility, still relevant in our soundbite age, to speak in Christ's name to lost people. We must find new ways of speaking so that people may hear. There should be a chain reaction so that people will hear unashamed good tidings, not chidings— leading to cheers not yawns.

The preacher's responsibility is not only to individuals, but to whole communities, that they may be shaped by God's word and mission. I myself grew through 14 years of ministry in central Cambridge to realize that it was at the point of the weekly sermons that the whole community, myself included, was being drawn into a deeper vision and commitment for service. At the beginning of my ministry the premises were closed for six days a week, when the city was most open. We knew that we had to change in order to do God's mission in the city. *And it was preaching that was to be the fulcrum of the vision through which the whole church had to be turned inside out*, to serve seven days a week. There had to be service beyond services. Eventually we built a centre open seven days a week, serving the needs of the people, with teams of volunteers giving the homeless overnight shelter, staffing a restaurant, providing job clubs and a counselling centre, and much else besides.

And I am for ever different because I had to grow in my preaching from *talking* about the upside-down kingdom in which Christ has reversed all that the world holds dear into *living* the upside-down kingdom as a whole people of God. Preaching and mission belong together.

PREACHING AS SACRAMENT

Peter Forster (1996)

There has been a widespread movement in modern Western theology, both Roman Catholic and Protestant, to bring 'word and sacrament' into a closer and more balanced relationship. This article will examine whether interesting light might be cast upon the underlying nature of preaching by regarding it as a 'sacrament'.

The term 'sacrament' came into Christian usage at the end of the second century, when Tertullian sought an appropriate Latin vocabulary to express Christian truth. He understood *sacramenta*, which he did not limit to a specific number, primarily as religious rites and symbols. In the case of baptism in particular, where Tertullian opposed the emerging practice of infant baptism, he also took up one of the original senses of the Latin term *sacramentum* as a promise or oath of allegiance. In later Latin theology *sacramentum* commonly translated the Greek word for 'mystery', and this fed back into the emerging concept of sacrament a sense of mysterious ritual, with a developing emphasis upon the eucharist as forming the centre from which sacramental theology radiated.

Although it was commonplace in medieval theology to identify seven sacraments, an official decree fixing the number as seven was passed as late as 1547, at the Council of Trent. Disagreement over the number of sacraments, and their nature, provided a fairly stable focus for Catholic–Protestant dispute into the twentieth century.

Modern historical enquiry into the development of sacramental theology and practice in the Christian tradition led to a widespread questioning of the restriction of the concept of sacrament to either two or seven specific rituals. Further historical enquiry into the New Testament itself has broadened our understanding of the range of activities in which God's presence is especially to be found.

The assembly of Christians united for worship 'in the name of Jesus' itself functions as the sacrament *par excellence*, and forms the primary context in which other less central features of early Christian worship are seen as manifestations of the presence of God. These features include the eucharist, baptism, the proclamation of the work of God, prophetic and hymnic utterances, speaking in tongues, miraculous deeds, prayer, praise, pronouncements of judgment and salvation, ordination and ex-communication.

It might be objected that even if such a broad list is to be accepted, only those activities that involve a certain degree of formal ritual can be called sacraments as such. But ritual does not intrinsically demand the use of material substances in the rite concerned, and there is a good deal to be said for the description of a sermon delivered in worship as a ritual. If the whole act of worship partakes of a sacramental character, can this not be said in a special way of the sermon?

To bring preaching within the ambit of sacramental theology need not confuse the specific character of preaching as opposed to baptism, eucharist or other 'sacraments'. The *kerygma* of Jesus took the twofold form of preaching and its accompanying signs and wonders, within the one proclamation 'by mighty deed and word' (Luke 24:19). The 'words' and 'deeds' of Jesus ultimately belong to the one category of *kerygma*. I suspect that many rich insights into the mystery of preaching would result from applying to it the perspectives of sacramental theology, but let me suggest three avenues for further exploration.

Firstly, the sermon is under some threat from those who would describe it as a mere 'talk' or 'address'. Granted that in the context of all-age worship a traditional sermon may not be appropriate, I detect that a rather casual approach to the task of preaching is all too prevalent in the modern church. To describe preaching as a sacrament of a special kind would at least serve to draw attention to its solemnity and importance within the life of the church as it seeks to live before God and celebrate his presence.

But secondly, an approach to preaching as sacrament should lead to a proper emphasis upon its down-to-earth humanity. Today the temptation is to assess preachers in relation to the superstars of film and television. How many preachers have agonized over the impossibility of meeting the aspirations of modern congregations, accustomed to the polished performances of professional actors or announcers? But just as the central sacraments of baptism and eucharist take ordinary elements of water, bread and wine and imbue them with transcendent meaning amidst their ordinariness, so the preacher must never forget the essential modesty of his or her task, and the need to devote our ordinary human energies to it. He or she should always be aware of the danger of thinking that formal ordination or authorization somehow guarantees a successful or adequate outcome to the venture of preaching.

Furthermore, the preacher who brings to the pulpit natural gifts of speech, drama and imagination is faced with the subtle danger of allowing these natural gifts to obscure the fundamental humility of the sermonic task. The task is to help the congregation to appreciate the meaning of the scriptures, as applied where possible to daily life. This presupposes that the preacher will understand the two horizons of scripture and the contemporary hearers, but it does not intrinsically require that the preacher be a creative wordsmith or a compelling public orator. Such things can doubtless help, but only if they are subordinated to the service of the humble witness, in the context of today's society, to the love of God enacted and embodied in our world.

This does not require false modesty, and is not an invitation to handle the spoken word indiscriminately, any more than should be the case with the bread and wine of the eucharist. Above all, the preacher is to be herself or himself, and is not to assume any false guise, be it arrogant, falsely modest, or merely parsonical. Whatever natural endowment the preacher will bring to the sermon, he or she will always and equally be a sinner of unclean lips. There will be good preachers, but not, it might be suggested, 'great preachers', or 'princes of the pulpit'. The treasures of preaching, like all sacraments, will be carried in earthen vessels.

Finally, the sacramental character of preaching will stress its immediacy. If the great flowering of theological and biblical scholarship in modern times has brought many blessings and discoveries, it has also brought its own problems. Chief among them has been the tendency to turn sermons into mini-essays or seminar papers which speak *about* God rather than *from* him. If this is often a particular problem with those who are fresh from theological education, it has had a pervasive influence.

Exposition may indeed presuppose exegesis, but it should not be confused with it. To expound Matthew, Mark, Luke, John and the other biblical witnesses to the revelation of God, is to expound the word of God as addressed to us today. The symbolic, but real, unity between the body and blood of Christ in the eucharistic elements and the body and blood of Jesus of Nazareth, upon which Catholic tradition came rightly to insist, must be paralleled by a corresponding immediacy of the word of God addressed to us in preaching.

It is only as, by the Spirit of God, the preached word crosses Lessing's 'big ugly ditch' between the contingent truth of past history and the eternal truth of God in his contemporary address to us that preaching has any ultimate meaning. The task of the preacher is to seek to be the vehicle whereby the Holy Spirit convinces the congregation that what the Bible attests is not first and foremost an academic but a living truth, not historical fact (important though that may be) as much as present reality.

To take bread and wine in the eucharist is not merely to witness to God's grace, but (in the words of ARCIC) to 'enter into the movement of Christ's self-offering'. To preach the gospel today is likewise to be drawn into that movement of God into our world, as the preacher seeks to speak in the name—that is, in the presence and power—of the living God, Father, Son and Holy Spirit.

PREACHING AS SACRED PLAY

David Schlafer (1996)

Animating every graceful sermon is an experience (for preacher and congregation) of the preaching event as 'sacred play'. If a sermon 'plays' well, it may convey information, give testimony, argue a case, present a poem, tell a story, promote healing, even, at times, gracefully entertain, rally, or remonstrate—or more than one of these. Those who listen will be so engaged that their appetites for preaching will be healthily whetted, even as their spiritual hunger is assuaged and their spiritual growth nurtured. On the other hand, when the 'play' dimension is missing, no sermon is likely to produce a hearing of the good news that is appetizing, nourishing, or liberating.

PERSONAL EXPERIENCE OF PLAY

Try to remember your earliest, most positive experiences of play. What did you do when you played? With whom, if anyone, did you play? Where and how did you do your playing? Give your memories of play an opportunity to swirl around for a few minutes.

Make some notes, or sketch some simple pictures of the 'play periods' you remember. Ask yourself: What physical sensations, feelings, and thoughts went along with these playful experiences? Why did you look forward to getting back into those play spaces at every available opportunity?

When I have invited preachers to do this exercise, I have seen them relax as they enter a world at once remote from, yet still very close to the current patterns of their lives. A retreat experience flowers spontaneously for these preachers in the midst of what was supposed to be a 'workshop'.

THE SIGNIFICANCE OF PLAY EXPERIENCES

The memories people have vary widely: organized sports, dressing up and playing house with dolls, playing cops and robbers, solitary reading in a special place, outings with parents, physical activities like swimming, sailing and swinging, the simple satisfaction of making mud pies—the list goes on and on. But what these experiences have meant to those who recall them much later is remarkably similar. People associate their play with a sense of freedom, which comes from a dance between *structure* and *spontaneity*.

Most of all, people recalling play speak of an utterly soul-freshening feeling that comes from standing simultaneously in two worlds, from creating an alternative world of adventurous possibilities out of ordinary, 'this-worldly' materials and interactions. These are 'new world' creations which, while made up of 'everyday stuff', still transcend, transform, and rejuvenate ordinary life.

Healthy experiences of play are neither frivolous, deceptive, nor escapist activities for children. Their capacity to deal with an adult world is rooted in their ability to play—to see the 'above and beyond' potential that is present in the world of the 'here and now'. It is not insignificant that a synonym of 'play' is 'recreation'. And finding adult ways to envision and enter new worlds is an essential condition of physical, mental, emotional, and spiritual health. None of us ever outgrows the need for recreation.

'It's just your imagination,' adults sometimes tell children who are deeply engrossed in the serious business of their play. The impression conveyed by such a judgment is that the imagination is somehow false or inferior to the 'real world'. When adults shut down their own imaginations, however, the 'real world' is significantly at risk. The worlds in which all of us live become prisons to be endured, or ideologies to be defended and imposed, rather than wonders to be adventured, and gifts to be celebrated. Science, art, growing relationships, peaceful conflict resolution—all of these depend upon the creative play of the imagination.

But imagination can be malevolent and destructive. 'War games' are often played by children as well as by adults. Jesus is definitely not commending children for their innocence when he tells his disciples that 'of such is the kingdom of heaven' (Mark 10:14). He may well be focusing here on the vulnerability of children as a sign of the radical quality of

God's imminent reign. Yet his focus on children is also instructive. Children know how to embrace play spontaneously. They bear particular witness to an essential dimension of the image of God which all of us share, and are intended to celebrate.

What does all of this have to do with preaching?

PLAY AND PREACHING

Preaching has more to do with the *envisioning activity* of shaping sermons then it does with any fixed sermon shapes, just as playing has more to do with the process of creative imagining than it does with any particular 'playthings' children produce during their 'play periods'.

One of the conditions under which play became 'no fun any more' for us as children is when one or more of our playmates insisted on doing things 'just the way we did it last time'. The alternative world that was freshly created yesterday is not a fresh world today. Play always picks up from where it left off—but it doesn't stay there. It may re-engage a tradition, but it doesn't dig a rut. Sermon shapes will have power only if they still bear the warmth and movement of the energy that has shaped them.

The child who plays is constantly shaping fresh worlds: the preacher who communicates the gospel is constantly shaping fresh expressions of the Word. But is it really proper to play with something as serious and significant as the gospel? I believe that the answer is 'Yes!', because the gospel can itself be understood as an expression of God's perfect play.

THE PLAYFUL DIMENSION OF THE GOSPEL

'In the beginning, God created the heavens and the earth,' the Hebrew Scriptures begin. The Spirit of God was moving over the dark and formless void. And God said, 'Let there be light.' God makes and celebrates new worlds. The basic narratives of Judeo-Christian theology can all be seen as celebrative bursts of God's creative imagination, which is neither frivolous nor malevolent. By breathing life into creatures of dust, God creates a world beyond the level of what the Divine Delight has just completed shaping. Then these new creatures are blessed, sent forth to be fruitful, and delegated the task of naming and caring for the other creatures that God has placed in the playground.

'The Fall' can be seen as humanity's tragic refusal to participate in God's game. 'Where are you?' asks God. 'Why won't you children come out and play?'

The whole of salvation history—provision for creatures now banished, a rainbow for Noah's family, a covenant with Abraham (and a gift of laughter to aged, childless Sarah), an exodus from Egypt and a recreation of covenant community at Sinai, incessantly fresh images of revelation that shimmer through the poetry and prose of psalmists and prophets—all of these are breath-taking fireworks of God's perfectly playful imagination, as God picks up the broken stuff of a sinful world, and refashions it into something fresh, special, salvific.

The Incarnation, the teaching, healing, reign-announcing ministry of Jesus; his resurrection from death, the new community he constitutes in sacramental sharing, the power of Pentecost, and the promise of life everlasting—all of these testify to a God who is constantly recreating: 'Behold, I am making all things new!'

If there is any 'case' being asserted here, it is not that God 'plays around', but that human beings play because they are made in the image of God. Gospel proclamation intends to help its hearers participate more fully and freely in the patterns of God's graceful play.

THE IMPORTANCE OF RESONANCE BETWEEN MEDIUM AND MESSAGE

If God is finding fresh ways to 'make all things new' then preaching that faithfully proclaims the gospel will need not just to say that, but to shape it. Effective sermons will make use of information, exhortation, inspiration, therapy, story, argument, and other rhetorical shapes and forms. All will be orchestrated in the service of the imaginative shaping of God's world-recreating reign. Good sermons will not simply offer us evidence, advice, or feelings about the redemption of the world in our Lord Jesus Christ. They will show it to us live and fresh—and take us to the frontiers of that new world.

A preaching student undertook his task with great earnestness. The results were consistently flat. In a chance comment, he revealed a major source of his difficulty. 'I read and reread my Scripture text,' he said, 'until I discover what doctrine it is teaching. Then I try to summarize that doctrine.'

The problem was not his commitment to theological awareness, but that he was standing at arm's length from the text, trying to figure out its puzzle, rather than immersing himself in its colour, its sound, its push-and-pull, its life. There was no sense of immediacy or relevance in his preaching in spite of careful inserted 'illustrations' and 'personal experiences'.

The preacher's Scripture text must be teased and tussled with as a vigorous presence, read aloud, over and over, in different translations, preferably acted out. Better yet, it should be read aloud and acted by a group of very diverse people; after which follows a discussion, not about 'the meaning' or 'the point', but the questions, the curiosities, the sensory stimuli it kicks off for different reader-hearer-actors. This process of 'playing with' the text is granting a living and active word the respectful hearing it deserves.

PREACHING PLAY AS A CONVERSATION GAME

Surrounding that central 'voice' of Scripture are the voices of the congregation, the culture, the liturgy, and the preacher. In effective preaching, these dialogue and interplay with each other.

In any game, co-operation is more fundamental than competition. Team members must co-ordinate activities, and opposing teams must equally comply with the ground rules for the game to proceed. The surface intent may be to 'win', but the deeper, mutually binding commitment of all contestants is to the making of successful moves—to playing 'a good game'.

The skilful preacher will, in her or his delivery, convey a sense of conversational interplay—a sense of back-and-forth. It is a dull game when the ball doesn't criss-cross the court or the field a number of times. Similarly, in a sermon, that interplay of movement is 'where the action is'. The energy and relevance of the gospel, the inspiration of the Holy Spirit, is experienced in the interplay between the different voices.

PREACHING PLAY AS MUSICAL INSTRUMENTATION

While a musical composition may seem to be reducible to notes on a page, the same song will sound very different if it is projected through a trumpet, an oboe, or a violin. Orchestration is an essential element of artistry in music. The preacher works with three basic rhetorical forms (not unlike string, woodwind, and brass instrument 'choirs' in an orchestra).

These are: poetry (in which sensory and affective images are predominant), expository prose (in which conceptual and analytic issues are fundamental), story (in which setting, character, and interactions are definitive). A music-like interplay of rhetorical voices in preaching extends the 'conversation game' analogy to a deeper, richer level of homiletical artistry.

Rhetorical orchestration in the sermon involves decisions as to when and where the preaching conversation will best be facilitated by the language of poetry, of prose, and of story. In any given sermon, while all rhetorical elements must be present, only one can predominate. There is a clear difference between the fugal interplay of brass, woodwind, and string 'choirs', on the one hand, and indiscriminate voicing, unpremeditated interruption, or sheer cacophony of voices on the other.

PREACHING PLAY AS DRAMATIC PLOTTING

We play games. We play musical instruments. We also play roles in dramatic productions which are themselves often more simply referred to as 'plays'.

Preaching is not stage drama. Nor does it have to be 'dramatic'. But good preaching always has a plot.

Preaching is an oral/aural art which, like a symphony or a drama, unfolds through time (rather than a visual art, which, like a painting or a piece of sculpture, unfolds in space). Whatever other shapes it takes, therefore, preaching must follow basic contours akin to scenes in a play, or sections in a short story. Sequence and suspense are essential elements in any sermon shape.

'Just what do you think you are doing in the pulpit?' Measured against the constant outpouring of God's daringly imaginative world recreation, I'm tempted to say: 'Not much!' But that entirely misses the point, doesn't it? Jesus never said to his disciples: 'Here's a parable—now you top that!' What he said, and still says, is: 'Follow me!' We can do that when we undertake the preaching task as an adventure of sacred play.

❦

PREACHING AS
A PERFORMING ART

Colin Morris (1995)

Preachers cannot avoid making public exhibitions of themselves, for in a human sense we are in the same business as the stand-up comedian, the actor, the politician and the barrister.

We have to face people, look them steadily in the eye and project ourselves, for as Phillips Brooks makes clear, preaching is truth conveyed through personality. A preacher may be humble and modest but never timid.

RISK

Preachers have much to learn from studying other professional performers. All great comedians have to be willing to take risks. During my career in BBC television I came to realize just what a lonely, neurotic and risky game it is to stand in front of an audience and try to make them laugh. A willingness to die the death out there in public, that's what's involved in taking risks in any professional performance.

The sense of danger generated by knowing there is no safety net in public performance gives an extra urgency in communicating directly with an audience or congregation. I just wish more preachers were prepared to take greater risks than they do. Nowhere in the New Testament is forgetting one's lines described as a mortal sin. The only biblical act of forgetting that is not excusable is to forget the one in whom one has believed.

INDIVIDUALITY

When asked what was the hardest thing about becoming a professional comedian, Ken Dodd replied that it was finding a distinctive voice.

It is faithlessness to try to obliterate our individuality as preachers because it's the only truly original gift we have to offer. Bishop William Quayle said, 'Preaching is not the art of making a sermon and delivering it; it is the art of making a preacher and delivering that.'

And yet, here is a paradox. The preacher having asserted his or her individuality must then forget, even transcend it. Morally and spiritually, we must be prepared to decrease in order that Christ may increase. Paul put it in a terse phrase: 'I, yet not I' (1 Corinthians 15:10). Preaching involves a form of creative contradiction. And this is not a matter of pulpit technique but of the preacher's interior spiritual life: it is an issue that is settled long before he or she enters a pulpit.

IMAGINATION

Preaching is an act of sustained imagination, though it goes without saying that we must not do violence to the plain meaning of Scripture in the interests of artistry. Once we have dealt honestly with the text and its context, then we can allow it to stimulate our imagination. John Ruskin once pointed out that the greatest thing a human being does in the world is to see something and to tell what he or she saw in plain language. To see, and then to make the congregation see—that is the imaginative gift, one of the central tasks of preaching.

In such a turbulent, confused time as this, preachers as public performers must wrestle with the big themes even though they are thrown by them. If we stick to the big themes we may have little to say that is original because we are following in the tracks of generations of preachers, some of whom left giant footprints in well-trodden ground. But there's no need to be deterred by the fact that it's all been said before. It is on simple, majestic bedrock assertions that our belief in a stable moral order and a consistent God rest.

The task of the preacher is all too rarely to offer a congregation a theme of startling novelty; it is much more difficult—to give new life and urgency to what is in danger of becoming hackneyed and stale. And this is where a rich imagination is required.

LABOUR

Though it is an art, preaching is also a craft and you master a craft only by hard labour, constant practice, trial and error, and the expenditure of much intellectual energy.

It is fatally easy for us to be slipshod and offer only half-digested arguments, illustrations aimed at emotional effect rather than specific illumination, material we have borrowed without acknowledgment, oratorical intensity which owes more to our glands than our deepest convictions, apparent spontaneity of gesture and expression craftily premeditated. We are taking the easy way out: we know it, and sooner or later the congregation will sense it also. At all costs we must not make great things small, holy things common or costly things cheap.

DURATION

Members of the congregation are entitled to hear an argument spelled out at whatever length is necessary for them to grasp it. The following through of an argument is hard work. So to omit steps in the argument or gallop through complexities out of the mistaken belief that in shortening the sermon we are sparing the congregation grief is in reality denying them understanding.

We should take whatever time is necessary, making the sermon as concise as is consistent with tackling the theme properly. Thoughtful people will stay with us for as long as it takes when they realize that what we have to say is important.

A CORPORATE ENTERPRISE

Martin Luther claimed that there can be no word of God without the people of God. The members of the congregation are not the passive recipients of our pulpit eloquence; they have a lot of work to do, for the sermon is a liturgical act. This is where it differs from many other forms of public performance. The word 'liturgy' puts the sermon in its proper place, for the term means 'the work of the people'. In the end, the measure of a sermon is not what the preacher says but what the people do. We act upon the church in order that the church may act upon the world. Indeed, as preachers, we have no access to the world except through the church.

EVERY PERFORMANCE IS UNIQUE

It may be a routine service before a congregation every member of which is known to us by name, but each preaching occasion has certain never-to-be repeated characteristics. Hence there is no state of spiritual equilibrium in which the congregation can remain suspended before, during and after the sermon. Once we preach and however we preach we will change something, even if it's only undermining or reinforcing attitudes.

P.T. Forsyth once told a group of theological students, 'When you reflect after preaching, "What have I done today?", say to yourself, "I have done a most remarkable thing. I have taken part with the Church in Christ's finished act of redemption, which is greater than the making of the world."' That's some claim to make about a mere performing art.

INTRODUCTION

Stephen Wright

What goes into a sermon? Part 1 has suggested some answers which should be taken as read: the gospel of Christ, the Bible, the tradition of faith. Yet these answers themselves pose further questions which are explored in this section of the book.

If the gospel is good news for each generation as it was in the first century, that requires that preachers understand not only the message but also their own cultural surroundings. Martyn Atkins' article suggests that this is more than a matter of dressing up a supposedly timeless message in superficially 'relevant' clothing: it is to do with interpreting our times with the insight of faith. He thus picks up, with particular reference to our 'postmodern' environment, a point raised by Jim McManus in Part 1.

Most Christians agree that the Bible should shape the central content of preaching. But should we use all parts of it, and if so, how? It is beyond the scope of this book to explore the range of questions associated with principles of biblical interpretation (though some models for the preacher's use of the Bible are discussed in the article that opens Part 3). Christine Pilkington, however, focuses here on one very important issue —our use of the Old Testament. She argues that preaching from the Old Testament necessarily implies that as Christians we enter into both the privileges and the obligations of being God's covenant people, and vice versa.

The theme of God's commandments is echoed in Douglas Cleverley Ford's article on preaching and ethics, a finely balanced reminder both that ethical issues must be touched on if preaching is to connect with people's lives, and that they must be dealt with in the context of a New Testament gospel of forgiveness, liberation and empowerment.

The next two articles deal especially with the language of preaching, the warp and woof of its verbal material. Geoffrey Hunter points to talk about God as the supreme case of our need for model and metaphor, symbol and story, if our communication is to be anything like adequate. Rod Garner takes this further, making a poetic case for the preacher to be poetic. Both suggest the impoverishment that results from trying to reduce gospel, Scripture or tradition to mere assortments of scientifically dissectible 'facts'.

Christian tradition can easily become fossilized in an unhealthy way, and preaching may, if we are not careful, become an agent of this process. The final two articles continue the theme of preaching's affinity with the creative use of language, and pose searching questions about the material from which we draw and the shape that we give to our sermons. David Dickinson argues that 'secular' literature may offer provocative correctives to 'safe' traditional readings of Scripture, and that its use in preaching may inspire listeners to engage in fresh ways with Scripture themselves. Dwight Longenecker indicates the power of myth to capture the imagination, and calls for preachers to find ways of telling the gospel story as 'true myth'. This will have a particular resonance with the changing culture with which this section began.

THE GOSPEL AND CHANGING CULTURE

Martyn Atkins

Effective preaching of the Christian gospel involves engaging not only with a biblical text but also with a cultural context.

THE IMPORTANCE OF UNDERSTANDING CULTURE

Few preachers will need reminding of the importance of proper engagement with texts. Engaging with biblical texts (and other texts that shed light on them) is largely and rightly taken for granted as indispensable to preaching the Christian gospel.

By contrast, engagement with the cultural contexts in which such preaching takes place has generally been treated with much less seriousness. Yet this is crucial to communicating the gospel effectively.

The good news is not preached in a vacuum, but to human beings who are located in a particular time and place, who have a certain history, language and identity, have certain experiences and needs and hopes, and consequently understand 'life, the universe and everything' in certain ways. To ignore or disregard culturally contextual factors is therefore, at least humanly speaking, to restrict the possibilities of people truly hearing the gospel of Christ.

'Engaging with the cultural context' means addressing similar sorts of questions to the cultural context that good preachers pose to biblical texts. 'How did this cultural context come to be as it is?' 'How might it be described: what are its main features, key concepts and core values?' 'What are the people like: what do they believe, how do they act and live, what is important to them?' 'How does this cultural context relate to what we understand to be the Christian gospel?' 'In what respects does this cultural context lie easily with the gospel, and in what respects does it clash with the gospel?' And 'what might God be saying through it?'

To begin to engage with such questions is to begin to take seriously the role of cultural context in preaching. A PhD is not necessary and a lack of formal academic qualifications cannot be used as an excuse for not doing so! What, then, are some of the characteristics of the culture in which we preach today?

THE NATURE OF CONTEMPORARY CULTURE

The cultural context in which Christian preaching takes place in Britain today can be described as postmodern and postChristian.

Cultural postmodernity is characterized as an environment in which institutions are regarded with hostility, certainty is viewed with suspicion, and ideological systems which assert that they have the answer to every question and conundrum are rejected as incredible. Cultural and religious pluralism is largely welcomed, and relativism—the view that one opinion, belief or value is as good as any other—overwhelmingly and often un-thinkingly accepted.

Such cultural characteristics pose searching but by no means insoluble questions for preachers who are popularly perceived as speaking for a protectionist institution, who tend to look upon certainties as their stock-in-trade, propound the Christian metanarrative, consider pluralism as a rejection of the truth of Christianity and regard relativism as sure proof of this rejection. By contrast, postmodern people appear much more open to certain spiritual and transcendent experiences, especially when they take place in a caring, affirming, relevant environment. They often positively embrace paradox and mystery, and greatly value authenticity, relationality and lifestyle choices—all of which lie easily with Christian faith.

In short, postmodernity is a mixed bag and good preaching involves sorting out wheat from chaff. This is the crucial task that contemporary preachers must undertake.

For example, if the church is perceived as arrogant, preachers must learn to speak faith certainties with both the words and body-language of Christ-like humility. If authenticity is valued, then what is preached must be incarnated—as ever, life and lips must agree. Rather than demonizing cultural pluralism, we should regard it as an environment in which the challenge of the gospel can be successfully made—just as the earliest Christians did so successfully. Relativism, however, will probably have to be rejected as incompatible with the claims of the gospel, though even then the mood and manner in which it is resisted will be crucial.

The people inhabiting our postmodern culture are often described as consumers and shoppers, posing preachers the question of whether or not the gospel of Christ can properly be presented as yet another product for sampling or trial—and if not, why not; and if so, just how? More particularly, if contemporary people are basically ignorant of the Christian gospel, and seek life before death rather than life after it, what are the implications for the content and tenor of preaching? If contemporary people value holistic rather than merely cerebral expressions of faith, then what does the act of preaching begin to look like and feel like? If contemporary folk are able to engage with what is proclaimed in a pulpit only when they start to know the preacher as a person, what does this mean for the social and friendship networks and lifestyle choices of preachers?

Inevitably there are more questions than answers here. Yet if preachers today begin to take seriously issues of cultural engagement, to look, listen and learn, and speak the gracious gospel into our contemporary context, it can again be received by postmodern people for what it is—God's good news, in Jesus Christ, for everyone.

❦

PREACHING FROM THE
OLD TESTAMENT

Christine Pilkington

On 27 February 2003, Rowan Williams was enthroned as the 104th Archbishop of Canterbury. Among the many uplifting aspects to the ceremony were words from the Methodist Covenant Service. These would, I believe, have gladdened the heart of the 101st Archbishop of Canterbury to whose memory this book is dedicated.

A one-time teacher of Semitic languages and President of the Council of Christians and Jews, Donald Coggan was continuously and passionately committed not only to the study of the Hebrew Bible but also to its use in Christian worship where, as the Old Testament, it needs to be read and preached upon if Christians are to stand any chance of being a covenant people. Sinai must surely precede Bethlehem. How can we possibly begin to grasp the wonder of incarnation if we have not first read Exodus 19? There God conveys to Moses something that is hard to encapsulate, but as a result, accompanied by thunder, lightning and trumpet blast, 'all the people who were in the camp trembled' (v. 16). The main thrust of the encounter is the invitation to Moses and his people to become 'a priestly kingdom and a holy nation' (v. 6).

It is here that we find the most compelling reason for preaching from the Old Testament. It is not only that we would be pretty well baffled if we erased all Old Testament echoes and quotations from the Gospel infancy narratives. It is that unless we begin to get some sense of this awesome God and 'take our shoes off' when on holy ground (Exodus 3:5, again on Horeb-Sinai), the immensity of his revelation in a human life will completely pass us by.

It is not a matter simply of substituting the word 'God' for the word 'Jesus'. Refrains of 'God, we love you' can be as inane as refrains of 'Jesus, we love you'. It is not a matter simply of whether you go in for this sort of song. It is a matter of whether some sort of content is given in the rest of worship to the word 'Jesus' ('saviour') in terms of God himself and to what it might mean to 'love' him. The Old Testament offers us the richest of resources for securing this content. It directs attention not so much to theological concepts which we can arrange under neat headings as to what it regards as the activity of God, variously as creator, king, father, redeemer, and chiefly as saviour. This last title for God cannot be over-emphasized, especially when it comes to preaching from the Old Testament in the context of Christian worship.

Attempts are made in contemporary liturgy to ensure that both the 'law and the prophets' of Jesus' own Scriptures are read. The Methodist Covenant Service is an excellent illustration. This service grew out of John Wesley's own emphasis on a covenant relationship between God and his people. In its latest form, in *The Methodist Worship Book* of 1999, it is explicitly stated that, before a reading from the epistles and then from the Gospel, there is a reading first from the Law and then from the Prophets (p. 284). From the Law, the lection is either Exodus 24:3–11 or Deuteronomy 29:10–19 and in response to the words 'For the wisdom that guides us', the people say, 'we praise you, O God'. The same response follows 'For the word that inspires us', after the prophetic reading of Jeremiah 31:31–34.

The question that Donald Coggan always thought was key is this: are we, the church, the people being addressed by God in the Old Testament? We must decide. If not, then let us follow the logic of this through to its conclusion and drop any claim to being the people of God. If we dare to affirm the covenant, taking to ourselves the words 'in order that he may establish you today as his people, and that he may be your God, as he promised you…' (Deuteronomy 29:13), then we must also follow the logic of this through to its conclusion and explore and identify with the promises and obligations that this covenant entails. This the Methodist Covenant Service tries to do. So, for example, to follow the readings and the sermon, there comes a beautifully worded section about God's making a covenant with the people Israel, renewing this covenant in Jesus Christ and, in our present meeting, renewing 'the covenant which bound them and binds us to God' (p. 285).

Repeatedly, in what is usually designated the holiness code (Leviticus 17—26), comes the succinct summary and motive for a covenant people: 'You shall be holy, for I the Lord your God am holy' (for example, 19:2).

Right through the Old Testament, if the beginning is always located in God, then the end is found in the human response. The roots of human conduct are seen to lie in relationship. As in the New Testament, God's undeserved love is presented as both the motive and pattern for action. Not loving your neighbour, in the ways spelt out in Leviticus and elsewhere in the Old Testament, is seen not merely as failure to observe an impersonal code but as disloyalty to God. To 'know' God, in the Old Testament, connotes both a knowledge of his requirements and a relationship with him that gives the impetus for fulfilling them (see Hosea 2:19–20; Jeremiah 22:16).

It is clear that we must avoid the false contrast of law and grace. We can and must preach the Old Testament law, drawing on the riches of the books of Exodus, Leviticus and Deuteronomy. In this law, we find not just principles but also consequences and motives. 'For you are a people holy to the Lord your God' (Deuteronomy 14:21) is not an optional extra for those who happen to 'like' the Old Testament. It is both a proclamation and a working definition for those who want to be the people of God.

In coming to a conclusion in reply to our central question, 'Are we "this people"?', it may be useful to recognize that the phrase 'this people' is found in Isaiah 6:9–10, which is quoted in all four Gospels with reference to people's rejection of Jesus' message (Matthew 13:14–15; Mark 4:12; Luke 8:10; John 12:37–43). Luke also quotes it at the end of Acts of the Apostles (28:26–27). Though it is there applied to Jewish leaders forfeiting, in Paul's view, their claim to be God's people to Gentiles because 'they will listen' (v. 28), it is salutary for members of any tradition, at any time, to remember that there is nothing automatic about either becoming or staying the people of God.

❀

THE PLACE OF ETHICS
IN PREACHING

Douglas Cleverley Ford (1968)

All preaching has to handle ethical questions, or it will not meet humans at their point of need.

At the same time, the gospel is not preached when all that is offered from the pulpit is good advice. Nor is the gospel preached when what is offered is a mere condemnation of evil conduct such as lying, brutality and theft. The gospel is not moralism. The gospel is only being proclaimed when the mighty moral power of God is offered.

We might express the matter this way: all preaching should be *biblical* (which does not mean that all preaching should be expository or even begin or end with a text, but it should be biblically based in no uncertain way). It should also be *ethical*, that is, handle ethical questions. Thirdly it should be *kerygmatic*, that is, offer God's grace to deal with the ethical demand presented.

The pulpit is not normally the place where *specific* guidance is given. There may be exceptions to this but they are rare. For example, it was probably right for the Confessional Church in Germany in 1933 and following to advise resistance to the Nazis, but those occasions are not common.

Most frequently it is positively wrong to give specific guidance from the pulpit. For example, it is not for the preacher to tell the medical profession what to do about certain surgical operations. Those are decisions that have to be made by the professionals possessing the expertise. Neither is it for preachers to give instruction concerning political issues. It is very rare for preachers to have access to all the relevant facts. Nor is it right for preachers to try to settle from the pulpit marital problems, because the situations in which they arise are all different.

The point here is that all actual decisions about actual conduct have to be situational, that is, they have to be taken in the situation.

Principles of conduct, however, are different. They have to be preached. An example of this is the Sermon on the Mount, and another example, Romans 13. Or we might say that preaching proclaims what Augustine said—'Love God and do as you like'—or, to put it in a less controversial way, 'Do in any situation what love impels you to do'.

Preaching therefore plays its part in the process of reaching decisions about conduct, but the actual decisions can only be reached in dialogue among worshipping people. This means in practice two activities: one, the public proclamation of principles in preaching; two, the existence of small groups, and perhaps the confessional, where situational decisions can be reached. The existence of this second ministry needs to be proclaimed from the pulpit.

In a way, formal preaching is at one remove in the matters of importance for ethics. It does not make the ethical decisions but it makes the climate in which the right decisions may be made. That climate is formed by presenting the character of God in Christ, and by proclaiming the preciousness of human personality in Christ.

Preaching has perpetually to undertake two fundamental tasks, namely, to make Jesus a real figure and to make goodness interesting. Preachers need constantly to be asking themselves if they are doing this.

One tool to this end is the presentation of examples of principles of conduct in action. They are not presented to tell the congregation what they ought to do in similar situations because all situations are unique— for the simple reason that the people involved in them are unique. The illustrations, however, are to be given because they not only show the way principles can be worked out, but also become sacramental points, that is, points in human experience through which the revelation of the Spirit is capable of breaking in.

In all preaching that handles ethical questions, the reality of evil must be taken seriously. This is what the traditional recognition of the existence of the devil was doing, and if it gave the impression of calling the devil a person (red tights, forked tail and all) it was really saying no more than that evil seems to operate in personal ways. It was not unlike affirming that God is personal. The important recognition, however, is of the reality of evil. We experience it in the dark recesses of our own souls and in the

❦

SYMBOL AND STORY
IN PREACHING

Geoffrey Hunter (1998)

'Metaphor—mere metaphor—is all we have to help us understand God' (E.W. Heaton, quoted in I.T. Ramsey, *Words about God*, SCM Press, p. 217).

In the first half of the 20th century, the 'logical positivists' declared that meaningful sentences may only be verifiable propositions (declaring that 'x is y', which may be proved true or false). But increasingly over the last forty years such 'logical positivism' has come under fire. It is recognized that each '-ism' or '-ology' has its own 'universe of discourse' within which well-understood rules for the use of words and sentences are established, and make conversation among its practitioners possible. There is no such thing as a proposition which is verifiable in terms that everyone could accept.

How, though, may we communicate beyond our own 'universe of discourse'? Scientists talk in terms of 'models', i.e. images or structures by which the matters being dealt with are made intelligible to others. Thus, we have learned to think of atomic structure in terms of mini planetary systems of whirling particles. Similarly, we must use 'models'—'symbols', 'metaphors'—to speak of God: we have no other way. By such means, we point others to what otherwise could not be pointed to. And we are doing it in such a way as to make clear that there is much more to be said than this, but which of necessity cannot be said; and the hearer or reader must go on exploring the hints given by the metaphor or symbol as it arouses echoes in their memory or experience.

'Story' can be understood as extended metaphor or symbol. The most effective stories operate at more than one level. The *Alice* stories of Lewis Carroll are memorable because they work not only as 'jolly good tales', beloved of infants, but at the level of adults, cogently modelling philosophical ideas. The 1997 televising of Joseph Conrad's *Nostromo* showed the difficulty of dealing with Conrad's complexity by having to reduce the not-straightforward story, with its social and philosophical musings, into an unambivalent narrative line. C.S. Lewis and John Bunyan appeal to all ages just because their apparently straightforward narratives can be read at other levels also, though they mostly avoid the perils of one-to-one equivalence at each stage. Conversely, the simplistic history of *The Story of our Empire/Railways/Royal Family* does not appeal beyond adolescence because it operates only at the level of factual recital: there is minimal reflection or ringing of bells.

The message we have to proclaim comes to us in the form of story. It can be thought of as the grand story which sweeps from Genesis to Revelation, or as the more particular story which tells of the impact of Jesus of Nazareth on our world. Into this story we are called as participants and purveyors. (We usually call this story 'the gospel'. Note the term: it comes to us as *good news*, not good advice or good philosophy.)

Liturgy is the dramatic and symbolic re-enactment of the story here and now. And preaching is the teasing out of what is significant in the story for the present worshippers as the story is re-enacted. It takes place in the white-hot overlap of Scripture (the authoritative expression of the story), the liturgy that re-enacts the story, and the life-stories of the congregation.

What then are the practical implications of all this for us as preachers?

First, story and symbol may be the way by which the word of the Lord comes to the preacher. Think of how the prophets are repeatedly asked: 'What do you see?'—and Jeremiah's almond shoot becomes a symbol of new hope; Ezekiel's rattling bones become a symbol of resurrection. Sight leads into insight: how and what the prophet (or preacher) sees becomes the way in which, as a result, the hearers likewise are helped to see into the heart of things.

Second, we must use story and symbol to bring the word of the Lord to others. This may be on a *micro* level: a single word may convey insight. We should not underestimate the value and power and colour of words, both simple and polysyllabic, both Anglo-Saxon and exotic. Or it may be on a *macro* level, through extended metaphor, pervasive imagery, or story. But it is important to use a multiplicity of symbols and stories (if not in one sermon, at least over the course of several sermons) as witness to the inadequacy of any one metaphor or symbol to point to the 'unsearchable riches of Christ'.

It is obvious that Jesus is the supreme example both of receiving God's word in symbol and story, and sharing it by the same means: 'Look, a man went out to sow'—and *that* man working on *that* hillside becomes the symbol of God at work now.

In the use of symbol and story, preaching is freed into a creative act akin to poetry. Preaching uses the tiniest of symbols (words) and their elaboration into metaphors, allegories, parables and stories as pointers to bigger signs which themselves point to God *at work now*. Then, by his mercy, the very multivalency of the story and the symbols may reverberate in the hearers' consciousness and bring to them life.

THE POETRY OF PREACHING

Rod Garner (2001)

Sermons fall stillborn from the pulpit for any number of reasons: inaudibility, scant preparation, poor communication skills, incoherence and plain old-fashioned dullness. The message too often appears to entail no risk for anyone and all of us know how easily passion and imagination are quenched by the requirement to speak regularly on familiar texts.

More worrying, however, is the sermon-bore who either on principle or by default continues to turn the gospel into a communiqué bereft of allusion, ambiguity or paradox. Devoid, that is to say, of poetry. Dickens' Mr Gradgrind lives on, and his obsession with 'facts' sits comfortably with forms of preaching that are only interested in explicit or tedious assertions. A heavy price is paid for this kind of preaching. It forgets that the gospel is not only what is said but how it is said, and it manages to lose the wonder of religion along the way.

Preaching, we might say, like theology, has value insofar as it points us to mystery. Jesus and Paul are pertinent here. Both are poets: the one is at home with parable and the other revels in paradox:

> *Impostors yet true,*
> *unknown, well known,*
> *dying, living,*
> *sad, happy,*
> *poor, wealthy,*
> *destitute, abundant.*
>
> 2 CORINTHIANS 6:8–10

Neither would have dissented from one of Emily Dickinson's poems:

> *Tell all the truth but tell it slant*
> *Success in circuit lies.*
>
> COMPLETE POEMS NO. 1129

The imperative to 'tell it slant' has always been for me a powerful reminder that our business as preachers is bound up with the poetic. This is not just a matter of the best thoughts in the best words (as Coleridge thought). What really matters is the morally or theologically strenuous thing the preacher attempts to say—the elusive 'pearl of great price' (Matthew 13:45) that lures us into speech and infuses blunt sentences with intimations of the ineffable. Isaiah seems to be aware of the necessity of the poetic in our proclamation when he comments vividly: 'Behold all ye that kindle a fire, that compass yourselves about with sparks. Walk in the light of your fire and in the sparks that ye have kindled' (Isaiah 50:11, AV).

We need imagination, because the heart of our preaching is in part a metaphysical romance with beauty and truth, and the ultimate source from which they both derive. Has anyone said this more eloquently and more passionately than Augustine?

> *Thou didst call louder and louder*
> *and didst break through my deafness.*
> *Thou didst shine radiantly and more*
> *radiantly and didst penetrate my blindness.*
> *Thou didst blow and I came to breath*
> *and life, and breathe in thee.*
> *I did taste thee, and I hunger and*
> *thirst after thee.*

Even on the cold page the impression here is of someone on to something important. Similarly, our own words need to dance, fizz and sparkle in order that the commonplace and prosaic might be transfigured into something magical, and the secret of Christ disclosed. George Herbert grasped the measure of the task:

> *Lord, how can man preach thy eternall word?*
> *He is a brittle crazie glasse:*
> *Yet in thy temple thou dost him afford*
> *This glorious and transcendent place,*
> *To be a window through thy grace.*

The juxtaposition of 'brittle' and 'crazie' in the second line is breathtaking. The joyful mystery, however, is that 'brittle crazie glasse' can be transmuted into something precious—a window revealing the graced possibilities of all human lives.

Words alone, of course, cannot effect or conjure this transformation. Herbert goes on to say:

> *Doctrine and life, colours and light, in one*
> *When they combine and mingle, bring*
> *A strong regard and aw: but speech alone*
> *Doth vanish like a flaring thing,*
> *And in the eare, not conscience ring.*

For Herbert, words fail to connect, fail to find the listener out unless they are mingled with and shaped by the life of the preacher outside the pulpit.

And 'there's the rub', as Hamlet said. Character, to a degree, begets poetry: it's the deeds and inner drama that we generate offstage, so to speak, and the depth of our intellectual and theological curiosity, that critically inform our word in season and incline a congregation to believe that the preacher has heard the voice of God.

James Anthony Froude, looking back from agnostic old age and recalling a sermon of Newman's, remembered that 'it was as if an electric stroke had gone through the church, as if every person present understood for the first time the meanings of what he had all his life been saying'.

As to the source of this magic, Newman was a poet as well as a preacher. The words from the pulpit were delivered with a beautifully modulated voice, spoken rapidly with long pauses between the sentences. No histrionics or strivings for effect: just that voice, 'subtle, sweet and mournful', as Matthew Arnold famously described it, and a piercing imagination fed by events, experiences and ideas that informed so much of his memorable sermons.

To read them now is still to be arrested by their power and vigour and the range of their concern. They exhibit a 'passionate coolness', characterized by restraint and allusiveness, but above all by colour and depth. In them it is possible to sense the poetic—the incessant struggle between light and darkness, the longing for the light and truth of God, and the rapture occasioned by the 'strange richness of everything'. Newman never stands still in his thinking. His heart and imagination are captured by the claims of conscience, the natural order and the immensities of the gospel. And they force him into bright utterance.

This really is the point—the extent to which we are still capable of being surprised, shocked, enthralled and moved by the figure of Jesus and this ambiguous world into which he came. Does the 'strange man on the cross' still evoke in us the pathos and the poetry contained in the following meditation that comes not via the pulpit but the agnostic playwright Samuel Beckett?

> *I am not moved to love thee, my Lord God*
> *by heaven thou hast promised me*
> *I am not moved by the sore dreaded hell*
> *To forbear me from offending thee*
>
> *I am moved by thee, Lord: I am moved*
> *At seeing thee nailed upon the cross and mocked:*
> *I am moved by the body all over wounds:*
> *I am moved by thy dishonour and thy death*
> *I am moved, last, by thy love, in such a wise that though*
> *there were no heaven I still should love thee,*
> *and though there were no hell I still should fear thee.*
> *I need no gift of thee to make me love thee.*
> *For though my present hope were all despair,*
> *as now I love thee I should love thee still.*

The sensibility at work here reveals that poets are those who are hurt into speech by faith, love and death, by the wonder that anything exists at all, by transience and time and the searing knowledge that although we are dust to the bone,

> *In that dust is wrought*
> *a place for visions, a hope*
> *that reaches beyond the stars,*
> *conjures and pauses the seas;*
> *dust discovers our own*
> *proud torn destinies.*
>
> ELIZABETH JENNINGS

SECULAR LITERATURE AND PREACHING CHRIST

David Dickinson (1998)

In the opening scene of George Bernard Shaw's *Saint Joan*, Joan is introduced to Robert de Baudricourt. She tells him that she hears voices telling her what to do. 'They come from God,' she says. He corrects her: 'They come from your imagination.' 'Of course,' she says. 'That is how the message of God comes to us.'

There may be several reasons for beginning an article about Christian preaching with a reference to secular literature, among them: to reinforce what I say, supporting my article with a literary authority like Shaw who was writing about someone who was eventually 'proved right' when canonized by the church; or to trouble or question what I am going to write about. Joan was executed because it was agreed that she was deluded, so my quoting her opinions about God and imagination is shaky ground.

These points reflect two prevalent views of the relationship between literature and theology. The frequent quotation of poems, novels and plays to support theological statements works on the expectation that God can be discerned in the Western literary canon. So we often hear avowedly Christian authors, like T.S. Eliot and George Herbert, being quoted in sermons. But the minority school argues that in the relationship between literature and theology there is 'a deep, painful and yet finally creative tension' (David Jasper, *Readings in the Canon of Scripture*, Macmillan, p. 11). Theology has a tendency to harmonize and define whereas literature allows disharmony and avoids definition.

When a preacher uses literature in a sermon, one of several problems may be encountered.

Firstly, the preacher has to be aware of the common objection that a literary construction is not 'true'.

Secondly, the audience's empathy cannot be assumed. For many people references to novels, plays and poems are a 'turn-off'.

Thirdly, for some people literature isn't ethical enough. For them, the fact that literature can be completely immoral or amoral is enough to compromise literature as a tool of theological reflection.

Fourthly, in postmodern Britain there is no definitive literary canon. It can no longer be assumed (if indeed it ever could be) that a British congregation is familiar with a common set of books and their authors.

Despite these difficulties, the use of literature in preaching opens the possibility of congregational engagement for the following six reasons.

It enables multi-layered readings of the Bible. There is always more than one way of interpreting a biblical passage. Alec Gilmore warns of the tendency of some preachers to assume that the biblical and theological scholarship of their years in theological college was the last word (*Preaching as Theatre*, SCM Press, p. 134). Instead he points to the joyful realization that the interpretation of a biblical passage varies according to who is doing the interpreting and where the interpreting is being done.

Literature (and other art) can provide the reader of the Bible with a 'fitting room' in which to try on different readings of the text as a shopper tries on different clothes to see which fit.

Literature forms a bridge between different worlds. One role of the sermon is to help the hearer make connections between different 'worlds': the biblical world and the contemporary world, science and religion, faith and doubt, the world of the present moment and the world of memory and hope. Literature can make the link between these various worlds.

Literature lets alternative voices be heard. In a postmodern world, faith communities that lay no claim to absolute truth are excited, rather than threatened, by the prospects opened to them by an awareness of the plurality of the contemporary world. Hearing alternative voices and stories draws one nearer the quarry in the quest for understanding and truth.

Literature troubles the canon of Scripture. Literature can liberate the canon of Scripture from the restraints of historicism and limited perspective (Jasper, op. cit., p. 126). In one of two recently published novels based on the sinking of the *Titanic*, a picture of the aftermath of the deluge from which Noah was saved is described. There are bodies everywhere. The picture leads the child who looks at it to ask whether God is evil (Erik Fosnes Hansen, *Psalm at Journey's End*, Secker and Warburg,

p. 14). Here is a work of art described in a work of literature which troubles the perspective from which the book of Genesis is written.

Literature also troubles the Christian story as classically expressed. It troubles the rules and insights the church chooses to pass on to its adherents through the filter of approved priestly pronouncements.

Literature empowers hearers. The use of literature in the practice of preaching encourages members of the congregation to become readers, writers and interpreters, too. A preacher's love of literature and the arts may rub off on to the congregation so that its members become preachers-prophets-interpreters who do it themselves. But there is more to this point than this alone.

Teachers often prefer not to lose their grip on the model of teacher as fount of all wisdom. So do preachers. Yet this is the model we must lose if we are to empower pupils and disciples. Giving students the courage to believe in themselves as readers is the task set before teachers of literature. Giving Christians the courage to believe in themselves as readers of the Christian story is one of the tasks set before those who deliver sermons at the Sunday service. In the way that readers are also writers and interpreters of the text, so hearers may be encouraged to be interpreters (what does this mean for me?) and tellers (what does this mean for others?).

'Everything that lives is holy.' This is what Alice Ostriker called the ultimate message of literature. To express this in another way, God is mediated to people by more ways than the Bible. The Spirit can inspire the modern author as much as the New Testament apostle. God, we think, did not stop communicating with his people when the seal was set on the canon of Scripture. Among the various voices of the world of art and literature we may hear the authentic voice of God uttering words which interpret to us what the church has chosen to call the Word of God.

MOVIES, MYTH AND PREACHING

Dwight Longenecker (1998)

MODERN MYTH-MAKING

In two 1997 polls of the best books of the century, the front runner by far was J.R.R. Tolkien's mythic masterpiece, *The Lord of the Rings*. George Lucas' *Star Wars* saga has not only been the biggest money-maker in film history, but has launched a new approach to film storytelling and won appreciative audiences worldwide.

Now that *The Lord of the Rings* is also appearing in a hugely successful screen version, and the church continues to wring its hands over the content and quality of preaching, we might do well to consider some of the film-maker's tricks of the trade.

THE PATTERN OF MYTH

Christopher Vogler noticed that the success of the *Star Wars* films was based on repeat ticket sales: people were going back to see them as if seeking some kind of religious experience (*The Writer's Journey*, Boxtree). His work led him to Joseph Campbell's book, *The Hero with a Thousand Faces* (Fontana), which considered the dream stories, myths and legends from civilizations around the world. Linking his findings with the psychology of Jung, he sought to interpret the myths, and discover the pattern of symbolism which they held.

The mythic story takes the hero on a quest. After the call to adventure and a refusal of the call, the hero goes on to meet a mentor, and faces challenges which culminate in the ultimate test at the 'inmost cave' where he claims his reward, and goes through a 'resurrection' before returning victorious. With innumerable permutations, this is a pattern of mythic storytelling common to all humanity.

Myth makes good movies because it powerfully draws each member of the audience into the quest of the hero. When it works well, the mythic movie is a minor sort of religious experience. This journey of discovery is one of self-growth, enlightenment, and ultimately of faith. As the audience bond with the hero they share his personal journey of inner growth and spiritual discovery. Campbell realized that 'the old teachers knew what they were saying', and told the truth not in obtuse religious jargon, but in the exciting and mysterious language of myth.

MYTH AND TRUTH

In his biography of Tolkien (Allen and Unwin, pp. 150f.), Humphrey Carpenter relates Tolkien's conversation with C.S. Lewis which led to Lewis's conversion.

Lewis had come to believe in God, but could not relate to Jesus' 2000-year-old death. Lewis shared Tolkien's excitement with myth, and understood how myth interests and involves the audience. Tolkien asked Lewis why he couldn't transfer his appreciation of sacrifice in myth to a true story.

But, said Lewis, myths are lies, even though lies breathed through silver.

No, said Tolkien, they are not...

You call a tree a tree, he said, and you think nothing more of the word. But it was not a 'tree' until someone gave it that name... By so naming things and describing them you are only inventing your own terms about them. And just as speech is invention about objects and ideas, so myth is invention about truth.

The light began to dawn for Lewis: he realized that 'the story of Christ is simply a true myth, a myth that works on us in the same way as the others, but a myth that *really happened*'.

For Lewis, pagan myths were testimony to the 'light that enlightens everyone' (John 1:9). They look forward to the 'true myth' of the gospel. The stories of incarnate gods, annual deaths and risings, all point to the story of Christ.

The Old Testament stories also had a symbolic, legendary and mythic quality, but they were locked into history, pointing, in a way no pagan myth could, to the myth become fact in Jesus Christ. In creating post-

Christian myth, Tolkien believed he was inventing another world which reflected God's truth. In doing so he contended that humans, acting as 'subcreators' in this way, most authentically reflect God's image.

MYTH CULTURE

Tolkien's work has sparked a whole new genre in modern publishing. Myth-making has erupted in a myriad of forms. A whole industry of books, films, video games and entertainment has grown.

Some Christians worry because they spot suspect theologies lurking beneath the surface, or worse still, they see the supernatural elements in the myths leading to occult involvement. The answer for Christian communicators is to understand the power of myth, and to unlock the mysteries of the 'true myth' which is the gospel of Jesus Christ.

MYTH AND THE BIBLE

The Bible story from Genesis to Revelation is the greatest 'true myth' ever written, sweeping from the dawn of creation to the mystic summary of all things.

The story of salvation history in the Bible follows the mythic pattern. Humankind—the hero—is called to adventure in Abraham, and meets the mentor figure as Moses and Elijah experience their mystic visions at Sinai. The nation of Israel overcomes tests, enemies and temptations on its way to the promised land.

In Christ the story reaches its summary as in him all humankind faces the ultimate test and the inmost cave. From there he defeats Satan, and rises again to lead us victorious with the prize of eternal life. Many individual stories in both Old and New Testaments take us through the same pattern of Call, Challenge, Test, Death and Rising.

The earliest Christian commentators understood this and interpreted the Old Testament with unashamed typology. Seeing the Old Testament prefiguring the story of Christ engaged the imagination and made both stories burn with a fresh relevance and intensity.

MISSING MYTH

While the Bible stories work mythically, they have more power than the pagan myths because they purport to be stories of God's real interaction with his people.

But the frequent Christian pattern in preaching and study is to take the stories, squeeze a moral or a theological point from them, and then toss them aside. From the non-use of these vibrant stories one might conclude that we would have preferred divine revelation to be a nice fat book of systematic or moral theology.

Instead God has chosen stories of full-blooded men and women engaged in the mythic struggle to overcome the forces of evil, find redemption and win a share in eternal life. Stories which are 'true myth' are God's way of communicating in the world. Once the mentality of myth is grasped, the practicalities of mythic-biblical preaching will soon follow.

IMAGINATION AND MYTH

The first rule of the scriptwriter is not to bore. The way not to bore is to make an imaginative use of conflict.

Imagination works on the truth to be conveyed and transforms it into a conflict in which the congregation can take part. This might be through the creative use of story, in which a main character goes through a process of discovery; or simply through imaginative planning, so that each point builds on the next and takes the congregation through a similar process. The sermon becomes a dynamic progress to truth through thesis, antithesis and synthesis rather than a bland statement of truisms.

These are also the means the myth-maker uses to engage the audience's emotions, which are the stimulants of action.

EMOTION AND MYTH

Soap operas, television drama, and pop music all tell us that emotion is more interesting, and more motivating than intellectual content. Even if congregations are interested in a purely intellectual sermon they are rarely motivated to take any action.

Preachers should not be ashamed of touching emotions in sermons. But this needn't and shouldn't be done in a crude and manipulative way. The wrong way of getting an audience involved emotionally is to engage their emotions directly—through cheap jokes, guilt or sentimentality.

Instead, we can engage an audience's emotions indirectly, as myth does. The audience bonds with the myth's hero, and experiences their emotions vicariously. This experience of emotion is cleaner, deeper and longer-lasting. Because we are one step detached from the emotional engagement we can be more objective about it. The audience member can also disengage more freely, thus involving the will in the emotional transaction.

This happens naturally with good narrative preaching. For example, we bond with the prodigal son, and vicariously experience his temptation, his sorrow, and the joy of reunion. The imaginative conflict in the myth engages the emotions, and once the emotions are fully engaged, the listeners might go out thinking.

INTELLECT AND MYTH

By encouraging the use of imagination and emotion in preaching we are not discouraging the intellect. Tolkien spent a lifetime making sure every detail of his created world was consistent and logical.

The mythic-biblical sermon will be a sermon about the interaction of God with real people. It will not be primarily theological but, as in Tolkien's theory, the story will be 'a new world' and thus a new vehicle for theological truth, and that world will need to be consistent, logical and intellectually sound.

If we want people to 'go out thinking' they need something to think about. A story of God and people which is undergirded by powerful theology and profound spirituality gives far more to think about than a theological treatise which neatly dishes out the answers.

MYTH AND WORSHIP

When the context of the sermon is the eucharist the argument for a mythic-biblical sermon is even more powerful.

Within the eucharist such sermons should lead to a climax where the story points to the gospel. The intellect will then connect the hero's story to its fulfilment in the gospel and the hearer will be brought to a closer bond with Christ.

The eucharist is a celebration of the incarnation and atonement, and the mythic-biblical preacher acts as a 'sub-creator,' enfleshing the truth of Christ in a story. The whole process reflects the incarnation and points to that mysterious union of Christ with us. The mythic-biblical sermon which engages the imagination, emotion and intellect will thus be the perfect preparation for Communion and that deeper, more mysterious transaction which is a sharing in the body and blood of Christ.

INTRODUCTION

Stephen Wright

The articles in Parts 1 and 2 suggest that preaching is an activity that is much too rich and theologically significant to be carried out according to any one narrowly constrained method or formula. Nevertheless, God is a God of order, and we are surely called to reflect that in shaping effective moments of encounter in the ministry of the word.

The opening article in this section focuses on the central issue of our handling of the Bible. It points out that Scripture may function in at least three ways in a sermon: as a text to be explained, a voice to be echoed, or a script to be enacted. The 'echoing' and 'enacting' strategies, especially, fit into the kind of creative approach to preaching advocated in the articles at the end of Part 2, but the article argues that 'explanation' still has an essential place alongside them.

Although some would say that all preachers ought to be able to preach 'off the cuff' if required, most would agree that preparation is both normal and necessary if a message is to be communicated with due clarity and cogency. Barry Overend offers a simple and memorable outline for practical sermon preparation, while Geoffrey Hunter and Leslie Stanbridge stress the special care needed for planning the kind of short homily or address that is fitting on certain occasions.

Preachers must take account of the other kinds of communication their hearers are accustomed to—not in order to ape them unthinkingly, but in order to consider the most effective way of putting over their unique message in an environment where they face much competition. Jolyon Mitchell and Roger Standing both draw lessons from aspects of contemporary communications media about the use of parable and image. They point out that Jesus himself gives excellent warrant for the use of such forms. They thus translate into a more practical key the discussion of story and symbol in the latter half of Part 2.

A question consistently raised over most of the lifetime of the College of Preachers has been that of the continuing appropriateness (or otherwise) of the monologue format for sermons. There seems now to be a wide consensus that the real issue is not monologue versus dialogue, but the ability (or otherwise) of any preaching event to be truly corporate, engaging the hearts, minds and wills of all involved. This may be best achieved on some occasions by a monologue using the kind of well-planned language, story and image discussed in the previous articles. On other occasions, notably (but not only) when a variety of ages is involved, the kind of interactive approaches outlined by Susan Sayers and Brian Pearson may be best. We may note here how much traditional British preaching may learn concerning engagement with a congregation from the culture of Black preaching.

THE USE OF THE BIBLE

Stephen Wright

The Bible is surely the preacher's richest tangible resource. Using it rightly, however, may be one of our stiffest challenges.

Doctrinal formulations of the nature of Scripture vary. Is the Bible 'the word of God', or is it a *vehicle* for 'the word of God'? How is it to be related to Christian tradition? In what sense is it 'inspired' and 'authoritative'? In practical terms, however, agreement is perhaps more widespread than one might think. The formulations may differ, but a high estimation of Scripture as the primary witness to Jesus Christ, the source of Christian teaching, the guide for Christian living, and a continuing place of encounter between God and human beings is widely shared.

Likewise, the challenges faced by preachers seeking to use the Bible wisely are similar, whatever preaching tradition we are most at home in. Whether—to use broad brush-strokes—our preaching is 'catholic' in its close linkage with sacramental worship, 'protestant' in its expository approach, 'liberal' in its aim to stir up thought or 'charismatic' in its prophetic immediacy, the fundamental tasks in relation to the Bible remain the same.

THE PREACHER AND THE BIBLE

What are those tasks? As an ancient text the Bible is to be understood on its own terms, without imposing anachronistic contemporary thought-patterns on it. At the same time, it is to be appropriated in the light of our heritage of faith in Jesus Christ. Its connection with the issues and trends of our own day is to be perceived. And its words are to be brought before congregations in such a way that, as they themselves perceive something of that connection, faith is sparked and nurtured, minds are gradually transformed, and lives are renewed. The goal, whatever our tradition, is encounter with God.

All this implies that the preacher has a daunting but exhilarating role to fulfil in relation to Scripture:

- As *biblical students*, we are to immerse ourselves in Scripture and whatever other studies will help us understand it, so that we may represent it accurately and intelligently to others.
- As *theologians*, we are to wrestle with the interpretation of Scripture in the light of Christ, so that we may help others to see its true Christian significance.
- As *cultural critics*, we are to observe our own surroundings, so that we may help others to see the ongoing relevance of Scripture for their lives and the world.
- As *communicators*, we are to be sensitive to the context of our speaking, so that we may order our words in such a way that the truth to which Scripture bears witness, both comforting and disturbing, may be heard.

It is a fourfold role that we cannot possibly begin to fulfil without the help of the Holy Spirit. He it is who ultimately orchestrates the encounter of God with people for which we aim. But the fact that he does what we cannot control or predict is no excuse for us not to play our part in study and thought, work and prayer—indeed, it is the motivation for it.

The matter of the preacher's engagement with biblical scholarship, theology and cultural criticism can merely be stated here. We may expand a little, however, on our task as *communicators* of biblical truth. I suggest that we may, at various times and in various combinations, do three things with Scripture in our preaching: explain, echo and enact it.

THREE WAYS OF HANDLING SCRIPTURE

Explain: This word sounds innocent enough, but we should not underestimate either its importance or its limitations as a guide to the right use of the Bible in sermons.

It is important that Scripture be explained, insofar as our capacities allow, because it is a strange text to 21st-century ears (Christian or not). How are we to understand it ourselves in order that we may explain it to others?

First, some quite straightforward perusal of a text by a preacher can set it in its biblical context. Then biblical scholarship (as mediated through commentaries and Bible dictionaries) allows many an obscure text to be cleared up. Third, theology allows us to see (among other things!) that many an offensive text may be taken as reflecting the historical setting of its origin, and may still illuminate (even if by contrast) the plan of salvation. Finally, cultural criticism allows us to see that many an (apparently) irrelevant text in fact has profound connections with life today.

Without such explanation, a congregation who hear Scripture read in church, or who read it at other times, may be denied light that could be shed on their path. Those who are at or beyond the edges of faith may hear Scripture as at best arcane and unconnected to them, at worst as mumbo-jumbo.

Such explanation is the main strength of the expository preaching tradition. But on its own (as indeed the great advocates of this tradition will assert) explanation is not enough. We cannot expect it, by itself, to facilitate encounter with God. Primarily this is because any doctrine of Scripture must reckon with the paradox of revelation and mystery. God has made himself known, and through our explanation of Scripture we may assist the process of revelation. But God is ultimate mystery, and there will always be that which cannot be explained. Explanation can help blow away some clouds. It does not, of itself, enable us to look at the sun.

If preaching is to facilitate encounter with God through Scripture, two other strategies of dealing with the Bible must be brought into play.

Echo: 'Explaining' involves being direct in our treatment of Scripture. 'Echoing', by contrast, entails being indirect. It means letting the language, tones and cadences of the Bible be heard as a part of the fabric of the sermon, rather than tackling its texts and themes head-on.

'Echoing' Scripture should not be thought of as a less 'biblical' way of preaching than 'explaining'. Indeed, it may in one sense be more 'biblical', in the sense that Scripture is not simply being treated as an object as it were outside the preacher, but is being woven into the sermon's language and structure. For example, a sermon may take the form of a contemporary narrative (whether factual or fictional) which echoes the structure of a biblical narrative which has just been read. Or it may discuss a topical issue, bringing the light of Scripture to bear upon it.

There are two particular advantages of an 'echoing' strategy. First, it enables the preacher to reproduce the classic emphasis of biblical interpretation before the modern era threw theology on to the defensive: that is, it enables us to focus on interpreting the world in the light of Scripture, rather than on interpreting Scripture in the light of the world. Second, it can evoke memories and associations in the hearers, strengthening their sense of 'inhabiting' the biblical story, while focusing conscious attention on some aspect of contemporary life that asks to be seen in a biblical light.

The main disadvantage of the use of 'echo' in preachers' use of the Bible is that it depends for its effectiveness, to a considerable extent, on hearers' familiarity with the Bible. This is something that, increasingly, cannot be taken for granted. A further danger is that 'echoing' can perpetuate standardized interpretations of Scripture, rather than a fresh reading of it. Since the main *focus* of an 'echoing' sermon is not Scripture, but the world seen in a scriptural light, the interpretation of the text itself is assumed, rather than explored or argued for. Well-known stories, such as the parables of Jesus, or images, such as the wind of the Spirit or the bread of life, may be used in a familiar and traditional way which may not allow a congregation the opportunity to come to a new appreciation of their meaning.

There is a tension here which is inherent to the whole process of human understanding. We all adopt (mostly unconsciously) some framework by which to make sense of the world. But growth in understanding necessitates not only the application of that framework to new experiences, but also the readiness to modify the framework itself. Thus an 'echoing' strategy assumes a basically 'biblical' framework for understanding the world, but if adopted to the exclusion of 'explanation', it could hinder—for both preacher and congregation—the process of sharpening up the framework itself through closer attention to the Bible.

Enact: To 'enact' Scripture in preaching does not have to mean a literal piece of drama. It means that the preacher so inhabits and embodies the text that not only is its meaning made clear, but its *force* is also felt.

Words not only mean things; they also *do* things. Above all, *God's* word does things. If we believe that Scripture constitutes a unique, even if not exclusive embodiment of God's word, we will want to help others feel something of that power in our preaching.

Hence I believe we need 'enactment' as well as 'explanation' and 'echo'. 'Explanation' opens up the meaning of Scripture, but on its own could leave the Bible sounding rather flat and lifeless. 'Echoing' lets Scripture shed light on the world, but does not necessarily give Scripture's *words* a powerful and prominent position. 'Enactment' helps people to feel the force of those words in their strangeness and ability to disturb, as well as their familiarity and ability to enlighten and comfort.

'Enacting' can be seen as the prophetic use of the Bible. It calls for an imaginative entrance—so far as we are able—into the original communicative context of the text, as well as into our own communicative context, so that the words of the text may speak afresh. For instance, as part of a sermon a preacher might declaim words of one of the prophets, such as Amos's colourful denunciation of injustice (Amos 6:4–7), followed by imaginary responses on the part of both Amos's hearers and hearers of God's word today (including the preacher).

On its own, 'enacting' would be insufficient, as it does not allow the necessary space for investigating the meaning of the text, or for shifting the main attention off the text and on to the world which the text is to interpret. Thus it is helpful to think of a balance between 'explanation', 'echoing' and 'enactment' of Scripture as necessary to a preaching diet over a period of time. Individual sermons, however, may well concentrate on one more than another, and this will often ensure a better piece of communication.

We could also explore—though we have not space to do so at length here—the appropriateness of the three approaches in relation to the various starting-points for a sermon. For instance, if two or three Scripture passages have been read according to a lectionary scheme, some explanation may be called for (especially of difficult ones!); but equally, some texts (especially familiar ones) may, once they have been read, simply be allowed to 'echo' in the sermon. Or perhaps there will be some 'explanation' of one of the readings and some 'enactment' of another. If the preacher is doing a sermon series following a biblical book, there will need to be plenty of explanation, as well as an element of enactment so that the hearers can feel the force and movement of the book's flow. 'Topical' sermons may be those which most bring 'echo' into play, as we let Scripture shape our interpretation of the issue to hand.

THE PREACHER AS EXAMPLE

The preacher's use of the Bible is critical not only for the effective preparation and delivery of a sermon itself. It also acts as an example for listeners.

The balance between 'explanation', 'echoing' and 'enacting' provides a good model. In our ministry of 'explanation', we can demonstrate the importance of wrestling honestly with the hard questions the Bible provokes. In our ministry of 'echoing', we can demonstrate the possibility of taking the Bible with us, in heart and mind, as a guide through the maze of a complex world. In our ministry of 'enactment', we can demonstrate that God sends forth his word with life-changing power— and that the ultimate issue for any Bible reader is not 'what will you do with the Bible?' but 'what will you let the Bible do with you?'

FROM JULIE ANDREWS TO JOHN WAYNE: THE PREPARING AND STRUCTURING OF THE SERMON

Barry Overend

'What man would think of building a tower without first sitting down and calculating the cost? Or what king will march to battle against another king without first sitting down to consider…?' Or what preacher will approach the pulpit without first sitting down…?

Few of us who are charged with the responsibility of delivering sermons actually approach the task totally unprepared. Invariably there has been a degree of planning prior to our preaching, but there is always room for a reappraisal of the preparing and structuring of our sermons.

There need be no mystique about the process of preparation. It boils down to asking, 'What do I want to say, and how do I want to say it?'

Paradoxically, spontaneity in the pulpit is enhanced rather than inhibited if we have spent adequate time in prior planning. Tommy Cooper could give the appearance of doing things 'just like that' precisely because he had planned ahead to do them just like this. Similarly, in order to preach 'just like that' we need to have put in the necessary time and effort to ensure that, well in advance of the delivery date, we know that we are going to do it just like this.

TITLE THE TEXT

In order to clarify in my own mind exactly what I want to say, I find it helpful to give the sermon an overall heading. This assists in resisting unnecessary deviations and irrelevancies. After hearing the sermon the congregation should be able to say what its main theme was. A slightly more offbeat title can occasionally prove to be surprisingly inspirational. How about a Whit Sunday sermon titled 'A Flaming Nuisance'? Think about it.

MAP THE MESSAGE

There are several legitimate routes down which to travel without getting lost. A sermon on the Feeding of the Five Thousand could take the straight miracle road, or it might head off in the direction of divine extravagance, self-offering or bread-of-life Christology. Selectivity has to come into play. Not every aspect of any topic can, or should, be covered in the sermon time allocated. Mapping the message route is as crucial as not straying from it.

THE CON-TRICK (1): CONNECT

You don't have to be a Julie Andrews to realize that to start at the very beginning is a very good place to start. It is a make-or-break place. To press the cinema analogy, if our listeners haven't heard the sound of music in the opening 45 seconds, they will remain tone deaf for the next ten minutes. Let them hear the tune in the opening bars and they will want to hum along. The congregation will then become our fellow travellers rather than mere passengers. The opening of a sermon needs to connect with the listeners through reference to a shared experience or to common knowledge. The hearers need to be able to say in their head, 'This preacher knows what she is talking about, and I know what she is talking about.'

An opening reference to *EastEnders* is not dumbing down. Depending on the type of congregation, *EastEnders* may well be a far better 'connector' than an erudite reference to *The Brothers Karamazov*. Remember, too, that Bart Simpson is better known than plain Barth! I accept that we cannot tell the Mystery straight. Nevertheless, we can tell it simpler than we sometimes do. Consider these alternatives: 'It's well known in agricultural circles that the final yield on a crop is often alarmingly disproportionate to the initial outlay' or, 'There was this sower who went out to sow...'

THE CON-TRICK (2): CONDENSE

Apologizing for an uncharacteristically long speech, Winston Churchill is reputed to have said: 'I'm sorry. I didn't have time to prepare a shorter one.' *Condense* is the second 'con' of the trick. Brevity, like topical or popular references, is not dumbing down. While mapping our chosen route we shall probably notice a short cut or two. They should generally be taken. It's not mere speed, but directness, which is of the essence. It takes Jesus seven verses to make his 'good Samaritan' point. St Peter's day of Pentecost speech runs to twenty-five. Which do you remember?

THE CON-TRICK (3): CONCLUDE

The parable of the good Samaritan is good news or unwelcome propaganda depending on which side of the fence you are sitting. For both sides it ends with a challenge. Conclusions, like openings, matter intensely. 'Go and do likewise' must long have rung in the ears even of those for whom it also stuck in the gullet.

To enable our listeners to take the message away with them, it needs to be brought home by a well-structured final flourish. Planned punch lines persist. John Wayne's *She Wore a Yellow Ribbon* ends with a tribute to the regular soldiers of the US Calvary: 'Wherever they rode, and whatever they fought for, that place became the United States.' You don't have to like the sentiment to concede that those concluding words linger long after the credits have rolled. Similarly, sermon endings should aim to reverberate way past the closing 'Amen'.

THE SHORT HOMILY

Geoffrey Hunter and Leslie Stanbridge (1998)

We firmly believe that in all Sunday services there should be preaching of the word, however brief the service and the sermon may be. Attenders at early or late services are seriously disadvantaged if preaching is not part of their diet.

The demands of such preaching are great. Clarity and economy are essential if a worthy sermon is to be delivered in (say) three minutes. If a preacher can do this, a sermon of fifteen or thirty minutes is in comparison an easy task. The task may be compared to writing a sonnet (14 lines) as contrasted to an epic poem of perhaps hundreds of lines. Mastery of short forms leads to mastery of large forms.

If, therefore, clarity and economy are to be achieved, a full text must be established (unless the preacher has exceptional skills of extempore speaking), even if, in delivery, only a skeleton note is used. At the same time, demands are made upon the congregation to listen and to work quickly and intently at the sermon, in the expectation and knowledge that it will not be a long one! In time the practised congregation as well as the preacher becomes adept at this.

A single key idea (word, concept, image) must be taken hold of. It may be from one of the readings or the Sunday theme, or an aspect of the liturgy or of Christian devotion and practice, or an urgent contemporary issue. Any material other than this one key idea must be set aside, or stored for another occasion.

The key idea must be led into as quickly as possible. In a familiar setting the preacher may well start without introduction. The idea is then developed with every imaginative skill at the preacher's command, for even within a brief compass there must be movement of thought and of emotion. Each word has a big weight to carry; the colour and resonance of words are to be valued. The sermon is brought to a crisp conclusion which leaves the key idea reverberating in the hearers' minds.

REFRAMING PARABLES
IN A MEDIA AGE

Jolyon Mitchell (1998, updated)

A skinhead runs down the street. He is filmed from three different points of view. It looks as if he is about to mug a man who is carrying a leather briefcase. Instead, he pushes him out of the way of collapsing scaffolding. Unexpectedly he saves this suited businessman's life. In this prize-winning 1986 advert for *The Guardian*, the copy is simple, but memorable: 'Only when you get the whole picture can you really understand what is going on.' This 30-second parable serves as a useful catalyst for considering different approaches to preaching parables in a media age. These can be summarized through six suggestions.

PARABLE

The *Guardian* advert is but one of a vast array of contemporary audio-visual parables. The narrative itself is rooted not in extensive scripts but in tightly cut shots. Such image-driven communication has become a common language today. For preachers seeking to represent biblical parables this provides both a challenge and an opportunity. The challenge is to recognize the popularity of this visual style of storytelling, and therefore employ appropriate word pictures. The opportunity is to use this form of discourse, to which listeners have grown accustomed.

In order to be heard in our media age, preachers need to develop parabolic forms of teaching. This finds precedent in the stories of a first-century Galilean, who, according to Mary C. Boys, 'spoke in parables because abstract, conceptual language inadequately conveyed the reorient-ation entailed in living in God's reign. The parables provided a means of engaging his hearers, involving them in a new way of thinking, and pressing them to a decision without provoking defensiveness' (*Biblical Theology Bulletin* 113, 1982, p. 86).

SURPRISE

Part of the force of the *Guardian* 'Points of View' advert is the surprise of what happens. Expectations are reversed, assumptions are challenged, as the skinhead rescues rather than 'putting the boot in'. Similarly the behaviour of certain characters in Jesus' parables would have surprised many of his original listeners. It is possible to imagine noisy audiences booing the tax collector in the temple (Luke 18:9–14) or the travelling Samaritan (Luke 10:29–37) when they first appear in the stories. But these characters surprise listeners by doing what is not expected of them.

The skill for preachers is to recreate the original surprising impact of the story. Thomas G. Long describes a parable's impact thus: 'As soon as we reach out to grasp a parable's seemingly obvious truth, a trapdoor opens and we fall through to a deeper and unexpected level of understanding' (*Preaching and the Literary Forms of the Bible*, Fortress Press, p. 87).

MOVE

The *Guardian* advert moves audiences skilfully and rapidly through different stages of understanding. Some have argued that the parables of Jesus had just one 'disclosure point'. More recently there has been a shift in perception of the stories. It is recognized that as we listen, the storyteller invites us to move through different views and emotions.

David Buttrick, for example, has helped many preachers to think critically about the transitions that they make as they preach (*Homiletic— Moves and Structures*, SCM Press, pp. 23–79). For Buttrick, concern about 'points' should be replaced with enthusiasm for making appropriate 'moves' in the sermon.

CHANGE THE POINT OF VIEW

By using a range of camera angles the director, Paul Weiland, tells the story of the 'good skinhead' from a number of different viewpoints. The line from the advert, 'Only when you get the whole picture can you really understand what is going on', can also be applied to interpreting and preaching on parables.

Reflect on Luke 10:25–37. Inviting the congregation to stand with the questioning lawyer, to walk with the religious professionals or to lie in the ditch with the mugged traveller, may help the listeners to experience the story more fully. Shifting the viewpoint, however, can be taken to ridiculous extremes, with expressions of what the donkey saw or the bird in the nearby tree spied. The result of too many viewpoints or over-idiosyncratic perspectives can be distraction from the original direction of the parable.

Nevertheless, as Richard Eslinger suggests, 'shifts in character point of view… are rich with potential for new insight and even new hearings of the biblical narrative' (*Narrative and Imagination: Preaching the Worlds that Shape Us*, Fortress Press, p. 145). Preachers have long employed such a multi-angled approach. A common rhetorical device is to lead listeners to different viewpoints at the crucifixion. The perspective of the gambling soldiers, mocking religious leaders, weeping women or cowardly disciples enables preachers to explore contrasting responses to Jesus' death. Similarly, in preaching on parables, changing the viewpoint enables listeners to catch new glimpses of the familiar. The goal is that it will draw listeners into viewing their lives and the world in alternative ways.

TRANSLATE

The parables were originally spoken in Aramaic, and were translated into Greek. This sets a precedent for preachers operating in our media age. A modern retelling of the parable of the good Samaritan provides a useful insight into how one form of translation could work. A Rwandan setting might also renew some of its original force. I will use Eugene Lowry's five-fold narrative structure for preaching (*The Homiletical Plot: The Sermon as Narrative Art Form*, Westminster John Knox Press).

First, 'upset the equilibrium'. A Tutsi lies in a pool of blood on a road out of the capital Kigali: he has been attacked with a machete. Second, 'analyse the discrepancy'. A UN soldier and Western journalist on their way into the city approach but then ignore him. A Catholic priest and Presbyterian pastor *en route* to a reconciliation rally almost trip over him by mistake. Pretending that they haven't seen him, they then dart to the other side of the road. Third, 'disclose the clue to resolution'. A former member of a Hutu militia in tattered old trousers kneels beside the soldier. She thinks of her own brother, killed by the Tutsi-led RPA. Fourth, 'experience the gospel'. She wipes the blood off his face, heaves him into her old truck, and takes him to the hospital. Finally, and perhaps most problematical in this interpretation, 'anticipate the consequences'. A mixed-race Hutu-Tutsi journalist writes up the story. His headline is: 'The Road to Forgiveness?'

This kind of attempt to translate a well-known parable into a contemporary setting relies upon aptly chosen pictorial language, as well as a tight narrative structure. Equally important is a sensitivity to the provoked different responses among Samaritan, Jewish and Gentile listeners, so this translation into a Rwandan setting would carry different meanings for Tutsi soldiers, Hutus convicted of murder or UN workers now based in a country wrestling to come to terms with its recent tragic past.

Inevitably, the listeners' own situation will influence how they hear and respond to parabolic communication. For certain audiences, outside the Rwandan situation, such a translation would not effectively replicate the original force of the parable. The result might then be a simple nod of the head, rather than a transformed imagination, lifestyle, or worldview.

REFRAME

The 'Points of View' advert is created around a sequence of different frames. TV news, likewise, creates frames around particular events, which help to concentrate the audience's attention upon particular images or stories. Inevitably this selective process not only includes but also excludes vital information. The second Gulf War, for example, dominated the news frames of the West, while the ongoing war in the Congo, which claimed over three million lives in the last decade, was usually entirely excluded. How a particular news story is framed also contributes to our understanding of the actual situation. Parables reframe reality in unexpected ways. Preaching at its best also involves the reframing of world events in the light of the good news of God's redemptive involvement in the world.

CONCLUSION

The most evocative form of preaching on parables seeks to recreate the impact of the original story, and of course many preachers already embody in their preaching the six suggestions discussed above, though not all are followed every time a parable is talked about.

In our highly competitive communicative environment it is worth remembering the 'genius' of the parable in overturning expectations or offering a surprising outcome to stories which we believe we already know. Thus, to adapt the commentary from the *Guardian* advert: With a parable preached well, it is possible to participate in alternative pictures of reality and be surprised into seeing what is really going on.

WORD AND IMAGE: PREACHING AND CONTEMPORARY MEDIA

Roger Standing

'HE WHO HAS EYES TO SEE…' THE RISE OF TV, ADVERTISING AND THE MOVIES

The present generation of 40-somethings were weaned on television; those under 40 continue to have increasingly sophisticated tastes as they consume electronic media through terrestrial, cable and digital TV, videos, CDs, CD-ROMs and the Internet. It has been estimated that people between the ages of 25 and 40 have watched an average of 30–40,000 hours of TV and some 250,000 advertisements.

Timothy Turner believes that this TV-conditioned mentality constitutes a real barrier to effective preaching. For him it has altered mental skills and listening aptitudes because it requires less concentration and effort and is more entertaining (*Preaching to a Programmed People*, Kregel, pp. 19–21 and 33). It is hardly surprising therefore that the 'That was boring' critique of many a teenager following a church service was overwhelmingly substantiated in a survey conducted by Gallup in the United Kingdom. Failure to engage with the implications of this prevailing culture has serious consequences for our communication of the gospel.

The situation is not destined to improve. Electronic media will become ever more sophisticated and of increasing quality, with an explosion of variety and range of available product options. In the business world, professional presentations will increasingly be judged not just by content but by the way the technology itself is used.

Third-millennial TV will not be exempt from radical change either. As technology improves, it will provide instant access to 100,000 films starting right now at the push of a button or 300,000 popular programmes after a delay of less than 20 seconds, all of digital TV quality.

In the light of such cultural change we do not have the luxury of simply perpetuating, unthinkingly, the forms of the past. Michael Rogness asserts that to preach in the same way as previous generations will be as effective a method of communication as a jerky old black-and-white silent movie in a state-of-the-art movie theatre with wide screen and Dolby Surround Sound (*Preaching to a TV Generation*, CSS, pp. 12 and 17–18).

'... LET HIM SEE!' THE VISUAL
IN THE PREACHING OF JESUS

A brief survey of the preaching of Jesus shows how he engaged the imagination of his listeners by using culturally appropriate stories, metaphors and analogies, and regularly varied his style of communication.

He spoke about what people knew, and used that as a means to open up the truth of God to his hearers. For example, he used insights gleaned from agriculture (Matthew 9:35–38; 13:1–43), the countryside (Matthew 5:25–34), the construction industry (Matthew 7:24–29), and familial rites of passage (Matthew 22:1–14). On other occasions he picked up on social prejudices (Luke 10:25–37), social customs (Luke 15:8–10), personal relationships (Luke 15:11–32), the experience of management (Luke 16:1–15), and of casual labour (Matthew 20:1–16).

Jesus was also able to deploy a whole range of preaching styles and strategies as he addressed his listeners. Sometimes he would begin by speaking about their personal experience (Matthew 16:2–3); other times he started with the Scriptures (Matthew 5:21–48). Sometimes he took an interactive approach and answered their questions (Luke 10:25–37); other times he asked poignant questions of them (Matthew 11:7–19). Jesus was an accomplished communicator. It was not just his miracles that attracted the crowd. The people were captivated by his teaching. While it is clear that the 'what' of the message and the 'who' of the preacher have an important contribution to make, the 'how' of the delivery of Jesus is frequently overlooked. The techniques that Jesus adopts as the medium for his message contributed much to the excitement of his teaching.

'OPEN THEIR EYES AND TURN THEM FROM DARKNESS TO LIGHT…' STRATEGIES FOR MORE VISUAL PREACHING

How can we respond as preachers of the gospel to the more highly visualized culture in which we live? We need to embrace new styles of preaching to open the eyes of those who listen to us. Here are four relatively easy strategies.

Painting pictures with words

Find creative ways to engage the imaginations of your listeners by the words you use and the way you use them. This is perhaps the simplest strategy to adopt, but it can increase the effectiveness of a sermon immensely. When you retell a Bible story or relate an experience of life, explore through your senses what is going on. What does it look like… feel like… smell like… taste like? What can you hear? It is through our senses that we build a full picture of what is going on around us. Just this simple strategy will help a preacher engage with a story through their own experience.

Using drama

Including dramatic sketches during a sermon is not new. If you have individuals in your church who are interested in acting, or a youth group who would flourish in their discipleship with more opportunities to be creatively involved in the life of the church, then this is potentially a fruitful path to explore. Sufficient time in planning is key. Appropriate sketches have to be both identified and rehearsed to be ready for presentation during a service. Drama done badly can detract from a service rather than enhance it!

There are many sources of good drama for use in church, but two excellent places to start are the Willow Creek Association (PO Box 966, Southampton, SO15 2WT; tel. 0845 1300 909; www.willowcreek.com; www.willowcreek.org.uk) and the Riding Lights Theatre Company (Friargate Theatre, Lower Friargate, York, YO1 9SL; tel. 01904 655317; www.ridinglights.org).

In the absence of a group of actors, retelling events from a recent episode of *EastEnders* or *Coronation Street* or a blockbuster movie is another way to create dramatic effect. It is important, however, to make sure that there is enough context and description for those who have not seen what you are referring to. Otherwise they will be excluded by your illustration.

Using video clips

Video clips can be particularly effective in bringing a greater visual dimension, but think carefully through the practicalities involved:

- Who will operate the equipment? It is better for the operator not to be the preacher.
- How will the operator know what to use, when to use it, how long the clip is and where it begins and ends? A briefing or rehearsal is essential to ensure smooth transitions, as is providing a script of your talk. Keep clips as short as you can (2–4 minutes is probably a good length to aim for). A reference document with information like that illustrated below can be very helpful too:

VIDEO: SECRETS AND LIES (DURATION 3.45)

from: 2:10.30.	Scene intro: After shot of three people walking
to: 2:15.06.	Scene finish: 'I admire you for that, I mean it!'

- How light will the building be, what do we need to do about it and who will make the necessary adjustments?
- How much context do you need to supply in introducing the clip, to ensure that it makes sense?
- Be aware of who will be watching the clips and seek to be representative in your selection, to be as inclusive of the background and tastes of your audience as possible. Are your clips too male- or too female-oriented? Are they all from action movies and not relationship-based ones (or vice versa)? Are they all set in the contemporary world with no period dramas (or vice versa)? Are they too white in a multi-cultural context (or vice versa)?
- Copyright: there is widespread confusion regarding issues of copyright. No church wants to break the law in these matters. With video,

however, there is no easy, centrally administered scheme to join, as is the case with other worship resources. Present accepted practice and informal guidelines leave a lot to be desired. It is important to keep integrity in the use of resources that are used. Current practice is as follows:

- Some churches have purchased Performing Rights Society licences (PRS), but these only cover the use of music. Others have purchased a Christian Copyright Licensing Video Licence (CCL [Europe] Ltd., PO Box 1339, Eastbourne, East Sussex, BN21 1AD; tel. 01323 417711), but this covers only a limited number of mainly Christian video producers.
- While it is technically best to write off for permission to the copyright holder for every video clip you wish to use, this can be a fruitless pursuit. Most do not reply as it is not worth their time and expense to write back to you!
- Many companies do give verbal consent that, if there is no charge whatsoever for the event and you are a completely non-profit making organisation, then it's OK to use video clips.
- Educational institutions are often copyright-exempt and it may be that some events could be classed as adult education.
- Many churches therefore endeavour to purchase a copy of any video they use so that the appropriate amount of money goes to the appropriate places. When taken with the fact that video clips can have a promotional value for the product and that churches are non-profit organizations seeking to explore and educate on religious/spiritual issues, this may offer a workable and honest way forward.

Using Overhead Projector (OHP) acetates or a computer presentation programme such as Microsoft PowerPoint or Adobe After Effect

While there are generational differences in the technology between OHP acetates and a PowerPoint presentation, they illustrate a sermon in similar ways. Tragically, with all the opportunities they present to bring a genuinely visual dimension to a sermon, many preachers merely use them to display words that they are speaking anyway. When using this technology there are a number of things to have in mind as you invest time and energy in constructing the slides for your presentation.

- How can you make this visually supportive of what you are saying?
- Keep slides simple and uncluttered. Less is more!
- How will people react to the image(s)? How can you interact with what is being evoked? Images that are too powerful might capture the mind of the listener so that they miss what you are saying. You may need to allow them time to catch up.
- If you are using words on the slides, are you merely repeating yourself? Do not be held hostage to the need to include every point you make in a presentation, or the thought that you must refer to everything that comes up on a slide.

Seeing is still not believing, but in our image-laden culture, having an eye to the visual dimension of communicating God's word will be a great help for those seeking a glimpse of the kingdom of heaven.

PREACHING AMONG ALL AGES

Susan Sayers

The first word that springs to mind is 'impossible'! How are we to communicate the gospel in a way that makes heart-sense to a completely mixed age group, with such a huge diversity of needs, lifestyles and stages of faith? Are we not bound to end up either in shallow generalizations that feed no one, or else focusing on one group and hoping the rest might glean a little?

We are right to be concerned. Preaching effectively among all ages is not easy, and needs extra careful preparation, 'proof-reading' for accessibility, and courage to experiment. But the fact that it's difficult has nothing to do with its value. If we go along with the fragmentation of community, splitting our services along age lines, how can we be a sign of the kingdom? Instead, we can turn the difficulties into opportunities for learning how to become the integrated community of love we are called to be.

As any athlete will tell us, it all starts with the heart and the mind. Think in your planning of unity in diversity, respect and tolerance across the whole spectrum, our need of one another across the age ranges. There's an inherent danger here that preachers will be tempted to fragment themselves in an effort to be relevant. Preaching among all ages risks being high on 'cringe' unless those preaching are prepared, above all, to be themselves.

If we had no existing traditions of preaching already, but only the desire to build up one another in this community of love, what kind of models might we invent to address such a gathering? It seems to me that the keynotes are our shared human experience, accessibility for all, and differentiation of response.

The traditional 'lecture' or 'speech' style of preaching is unlikely to be accessible for mixed ages as it stands. Ways of making such preaching more accessible include visuals, using ready-made or 'draw as you go' visual commentaries, projected pictures, and three-dimensional metaphors alongside the sermon. Downloaded clip-art is helpful here, as well as very localized images that are immediately relevant, grounding the teaching in the particular area around the church. In the same way, spoken examples need to be drawn from the different experiences of the ages present, so that everyone can apply what is being said to their own situation. Right-brained people (of any age) may find it helpful to have pencils or crayons and paper available as they listen and respond.

But we can also preach in many other ways apart from that adapted traditional model. A rehearsed 'things of God' conversation, for instance, can teach not only through its content but also in modelling ways of talking about such deeply important matters as love, forgiveness, prayer and faith. A carefully planned public discussion within a mixed age group can also be helpful, provided the microphone is passed around those speaking.

Alternatively, the talk can be punctuated with a couple of (very short) opportunities for either sharing thoughts with those sitting near each other, or thinking through them alone. Such an invited response needs to be introduced very specifically, with the point to be discussed displayed simply and with a symbol or icon. This allows people to talk across or within the age groups, so that a natural differentiation of response happens.

The preaching can be broken into two or three more manageable short chunks, with perhaps a visual being added each time, so that continuity is maintained. It can take the form of story, with an opportunity for questions and responses given afterwards over refreshments, or as part of the service. Members of the congregation can be involved in the telling or the exploration, and it's quite important that this involvement is not seen as something only the children do. Having a mix of ages involved in the talk speaks visibly of the community we claim to be.

And what of those who have babies and young toddlers with them? The ongoing message is being preached here in the active care and love that provides a warm, safe environment, shares the nurture, and ensures that those behind any glass partitions are still able to hear and take part—parents with young children are quite used to multi-tasking.

Preaching among all ages is about celebrating the diversity within the community, and homing in on the opportunities it offers rather than the problems it raises.

INTERACTIVE METHODS OF PREACHING

Brian Pearson

As I entered the room and moved to sit opposite him, the man I looked upon was clearly tired and frail. As he slowly unpeeled a banana he began our conversation by apologizing. 'If I doze off,' he said, 'don't take it personally. I'm inclined to do that these days.' We spent 45 minutes together—and he didn't doze off! In fact, his energy appeared to increase as the time passed and as he became more involved in recounting experiences associated with a favourite subject—preaching.

The man was Lord Soper and he had recently turned 90. Although we covered some personal background, the interview really 'took off' when he relived the excitement and the fun of public preaching. And this excitement and fun was never more apparent than when he stepped up on to his 'Soper-box' at Hyde Park Corner. He was well into his stride, when I asked, 'What about the hecklers? Weren't they a problem?'

'Problem?' he replied. 'Not at all. They were an asset!' It was then I realized that I was about to receive my first insight into 'interactive preaching'.

'Interactive' preaching is but one kind of 'participative' preaching. The preacher will hope that everyone listening to his/her address will be 'participating' in so far as they are listening, processing and reflecting upon the words that flow. But without being too precise in terminology, we know that there is a considerable difference between 'passive partici-pation' and 'active participation'.

There is a further difference, though, between 'active participation' and 'interaction'—at least, in my book there is! 'Participation' allows the preacher to retain a considerable amount of control over content and direction. Other people may become the supporting cast or extras but they are unlikely to be the script writers or editors. 'Interaction' allows a shift in, or partial relinquishing of, control—and therein, for the bold preacher, lies the seductive element of risk.

I offer a sweeping statement—which I will not take time to defend here—about contemporary culture. It expects to be invited to participate, to be an active stakeholder; and if that offer is not forthcoming then there will always be alternative attractions to pursue. Add to this the limited attention span now associated with non-participative activities and we begin to appreciate that a growing proportion of our congregations need different vehicles to allow them to engage with a preacher. Some of these vehicles may be found in the 'Interactive Methods' depot.

Meanwhile, back with Lord Soper: why exactly was the heckler so valuable? He or she was the sounding board, the spokesperson, the *vox pop*, the yeast, and the voice of the relevant. The heckler had an agenda— even if teasing it out was an art—and it was often an agenda shared by others standing by. By addressing that agenda as a priority, the sermon could move to a quite different order of impact. How often have some brilliantly constructed and presented sermons fallen short on account of answering questions that are not being asked, providing solutions to problems that are not recognized?

Of course, not all of Lord Soper's hecklers were so helpful. He had his fair share of both personal abuse and those vying with him for centre stage—that was part of the risk of being on that particular platform and embracing a particular style—but, for Soper, the benefits far outweighed the costs. I would not attempt to encourage anyone to emulate his or any other method, but rather to explore the possibilities of a more interactive approach within the context and style of our own preaching.

So let us consider some other examples of interactive preaching, while holding to the basic principles, and the inherent risk.

Some years ago, I discovered that if, after preaching, I had a conversation with a person who had read the passage on which I had preached, then I would almost invariably have a more informed and lively discussion than with other members of the congregation. It was not the sole factor, of course, but the reader would, it seemed, because of his/her prior engagement with the relevant passage, be equipped to engage with the piece as a whole rather with than a single or couple of strands of thinking. What struck me was this: why leave that lively interaction until the post-service cuppa? Why could not that valuable dynamic become an integral part of the service—even an integral part of the sermon? True, the means must be devised according to a whole range of contextual factors, but the principle, I suggest, is one worthy of further exploration.

To go a step further, there may be an inbuilt assumption (self-imposed limitation?) that the interaction is one that primarily involves the preacher. I am a keen cricketer and one of the warm-up exercises I should perform (but often manage to avoid!) is the circle bat-catch. One player in the middle of a circle made up of other players has a bat with which he hits the ball at catchable height in random sequence to his colleagues. They toss it back, and so on. It is quite effective as a routine, but note that everything revolves around the guy in the middle. The interaction is a series of one-to-ones through the nominal leader. Take the middleman out and let the ball fly randomly around and across the circle, and a different dynamic emerges. The process is sharper, less predictable; participants remain more focused. Set several balls loose at once and... well, OK, you could end up with several players injured before the match even starts—which is a timely reminder never to press an illustration beyond its natural limits!

Now a rather different approach. In recent months I have been experimenting with (for me) a new style. Thus far I have employed it in a very limited way. I admit to lacking in some confidence as yet (and probably a considerable amount of competence as well!) but I want to persevere and hone this new style to the extent that I will be able to judge whether it is 'for me' or not. I don't do gimmicks, but I do take professional development seriously, and that inevitably means trying things out and being prepared to shape and improve them before adopting or ditching them.

In my case, I am employing dramatic presentation by inviting members of the congregation to become a part of the story that is presented within the fabric of the sermon. The risky bit is when, having set up the scene and allowed the story to unfold, I involve the 'actors' in a more interactive way. I will ask them what they think is going on, why their character is behaving in a certain way, what the character might be feeling, and where this might lead. The technique is not new in the context of Bible study but it has not, in my experience, been over-employed in preaching. I have found it a very exciting medium. Not only does it give rise very easily to later conversations, but far from all of those con-versations are with me. People want to talk with the 'characters'. The observers too have been drawn into the scene. The sermon lives on!

The mind is a stunningly brilliant bit of kit. One feature that intrigues

INTRODUCTION

Stephen Wright

Preaching may take place in a great variety of settings. This section opens with substantial considerations of two of the 'macro' contexts for preaching—preaching among the faithful at worship, and preaching to unbelievers. It moves to two practical treatments of some of the specific 'micro' contexts in which we find ourselves, occasional services at which the two 'macro' contexts overlap, for there we preach within worship but often to many who do not yet believe. It concludes with two pieces reflecting on the particular challenges of preaching in the midst of suffering and crisis.

The first two articles form a pair with those on 'Preaching as sacrament' and 'Preaching as a missionary activity' in Part 1. Ian Paton argues that preaching most fittingly occurs within worship, and is thereby saved from over-grandiose claims for itself. It is interesting that in the practice of the church this does not preclude preaching being taken beyond the walls of a building where the faithful are gathered. From Roman Catholic *Corpus Christi* processions to charismatic 'Marches for Jesus', public proclamation entails acts of worship as well as acts of preaching. Lesslie Newbigin's account of apologetic preaching, conversely, may be equally applicable to many 'in-church' occasions as it is to conversations or addresses outside the church walls, for the model of storytelling that he commends as the key tool for faith-sharing in our time is very much at home in precisely the regular round of liturgical worship that Ian Paton describes. The key must be to let the stories be accessible to those who are not yet familiar with them.

Services of initiation, rites of passage and civic occasions constitute frontier territory for the preacher, when we come into contact simultaneously with belief, half-belief and unbelief, in a context of complex emotions. Geoffrey Hunter, Richard Broadberry and Michael Henshall help us to see some of the skills needed for suitable preaching at these times.

Human suffering and crisis, and the suffering of Christ himself at the heart of our gospel, pose perhaps the ultimate challenge for the preacher, making us ask whether to utter anything at all is to trespass upon a necessary silence. Rod Garner helps us to tread this delicate line between the need to speak and the inadequacy of words to match painful truth. Paul Johns, meanwhile, links our call to be interpreters of the crises of our times to the theme of storytelling which has been a consistent thread of this section, this book, and the discussion of preaching over the last few decades.

PREACHING AND WORSHIP

Ian Paton (2002)

THE NATURE OF WORSHIP

What is worship? Worship is, first of all, adoration. *Adorare* means 'to pray towards'—a word full of dynamism and movement and yearning.

Worship is something done before it is something said. Worship is action. It is the word proclaimed and heard, of course, but it is more than that. Music, movement, ritual (i.e. patterned symbolic behaviour), silence, are just as much part of it. Liturgical worship is a living presentation of the word of God, its translation into deed—symbolic ritual deed, but deed nonetheless.

Preaching is part of this pattern of doing and speaking, moving and hearing. The liturgical sermon is not a free-floating moment of preaching. It should flow quite naturally out of the readings and into the liturgical action that follows. Seeing it this way may help us to avoid two extremes: first, that the sermon should carry the entire weight of the worship experience, and remain alone responsible for interpreting the experience of faith; and second, that preaching should have instant results. We can trust God's word to do its work week by week in forming the people of God through their regular worship.

THE SIGNIFICANCE OF THE CHRISTIAN CALENDAR

For instance, the liturgical year, expressed in the ecumenical and international Revised Common Lectionary, is a valuable aid to psychological and spiritual formation. *Psychological* formation because expectancy, joy, and awe are cultivated during the Advent–Christmas–Epiphany season;

fear, sorrow, hope, and strengthening during the Lent–Easter–Pentecost season; faithful, persevering growth in love marks Ordinary Time. *Spiritual* formation because we are invited to acknowledge the coming of God in Jesus (Advent–Christmas–Epiphany). We contemplate Jesus' death, resurrection, and sending of the Spirit (Lent–Easter–Pentecost). We reflect on the daily life of Jesus, in order to see the Father at work in Jesus' life and ours (ordinary time).

This unfolding of the mystery of salvation occurs through the lectionary but also through the prayers and psalms and hymns of the liturgy. We are presented through the year with every aspect of Jesus' life, death, and glorification—indeed, with all that Jesus said and did. We hear his parables, his challenges, his warnings, his encouragements.

This formative influence of the liturgical year is subtle, because usually we scarcely notice it. To help someone around Christmas time to work through a challenge in their life, a spiritual director suggests meditation on Mary's 'Yes' to God, rather than on Jesus' word in the Garden of Gethsemane, 'Not my will but yours be done.' A retreat director during Holy Week does not focus her guidance on God's coming in the flesh in the form of an infant, but on God's immense love manifested in death and resurrection.

The liturgy operates by supplying its participants with data—external data in the form of impressions on the senses and internal data in the form of evoked images and feelings. It does this in such a way as to lead to insights, judgments, and decisions in regard to life and death, repentance and faith, serving our neighbours. These juxtapositions, these data, are not all on the conscious level. As we know from experience, a film, a drama, or even a conversation has an impact upon us which we do not recognize at the time; we may discern it only days or weeks later.

Furthermore, during the course of a year, the liturgy is doing this against the backdrop of the events of history, our own personal stories and that of the world. It constantly raises the question, which it is the liturgical preacher's task to pose time after time: 'How do we think of Jesus at the same time as, say, the killing grounds of the Middle East? How do we speak in the same sentence of Jesus and cancer, Jesus and refugees, Jesus and Al Qaeda?'

PREACHING WITHIN THE LITURGY

David Edwards in *The Futures of Christianity* (Hodder & Stoughton, p. 13) wrote: 'We are the primitive Church.' He did not mean that we were recovering or re-living the vision of early Christians. He meant we *are* the early church, because it is only 2000 years old: we are still in the early days of Christianity, looking about, wrestling with a faith we have been given, finding out what we should do with it.

Liturgical preaching is an activity carried on from within a worshipping community that sees itself as contemporary with the life of Israel and the early church. The life of this congregation and the lives of those long-dead believers is the same life, for this is the same people. An awareness of this dimension on the part of preachers speaking in a worship context will be conveyed only if they have this understanding. It is a matter of what the Passover Seder says at the offering of the cup of remembrance of the Exodus: 'Not only our ancestors were redeemed by God from slavery; all of us are now redeemed in spirit and example. Each of us, each generation, is a beneficiary of God's power of salvation. For this reason we raise our cup and drink the wine of remembrance.' It is a matter of doing with the word what Jesus Christ asked his disciples to do with bread and cup: 'Do this for the remembrance of me.' The word, as much as the sacrament, is a matter of *remembrance*—a matter of situating the events of salvation not just in past history but in the history that is the present moment.

So the Scriptures are books about relationships and communities, economics and politics. The Evangelists do not much care if the event happened to Levi or Zacchaeus or Matthew. They wish to reach their own contemporaries, and through them, all of us. Liturgical preaching strives to do what the liturgy strives to do: to convince hearers of their solidarity in faith—or lack of faith—with the people of the Bible. Adam and Eve, Cain and Abel, become the worshippers' contemporaries. The Bible, as Richard Holloway has said, is not *history*, it is *our story*.

The liturgical sermon's great advantage in facilitating this is precisely its ritual context. Preaching need not rely solely on its own 'power'. Once the ritual has ended, the congregation has not only heard, but also seen, felt, smelled, and tasted an alternative world. For instance, in a world of inequality and injustice, the ritual that proclaims justice for all in the kingdom of God, the eucharist, also performs that justice, in the sharing of bread and wine, without distinction and without price.

At its best, preaching has helped to make this alternative world accessible to *this* people, at *this* time, in *this* place. As Rowan Williams puts it, 'We are transformed because our horizons have broadened; we see differently because at least *some* of the co-ordinates by which we situate ourselves have been altered.'

Liturgical preaching only really makes sense when it is one with its context, the mystery of worship. Out of that context, or paying no attention to that context, it may just sound like the self-conscious thinking-aloud of a church that is trying to impress: opinionated and a little ridiculous. The 1930s Archbishop of Canterbury said to Hensley Henson, 'You really must come and hear me preach.' Henson famously replied, 'I have never heard your Grace doing anything else.'

⚸

APOLOGETIC PREACHING

Lesslie Newbigin (1993)

Our subject is preaching which seeks to enable unbelievers, or half-believers, to come to belief.

THE CUL-DE-SAC OF NATURAL THEOLOGY

There is a tradition which says: 'Start where they are'. It is right that we use language, models, images, concepts with which the hearers are at home, so that they can 'latch on to' what we are saying. But it is wrong to suppose that there are some universally obvious truths *from which* we can argue the case for Christianity. There is a very long tradition of 'natural theology' which lays a philosophical foundation on which you build a theological super-structure. Why do I say that this is wrong?

It is notorious that the 'proofs' of the existence of God, for example, are not conclusive. One can use this method to show that belief in God is possible, but not to provide certainty. Moreover, the 'God' whose existence is proved by natural theology is never recognizable as the God of the Bible. Remember the words on the scrap of paper found sewn up inside Pascal's jacket: 'Fire! Not the god of the philosophers: the God of Abraham, of Isaac and of Jacob.'

The question has to be put sharply: Is the 'God' of natural theology a step on the way to belief in the true God, or a step in the wrong direction? Is it, indeed, precisely an idol, a construct, not of human hands, but of human brains? The difficulty many have with the doctrine of the Incarnation suggests that 'natural theology' is a blind alley. Many find it impossible to believe that God could be a baby lying in a manger, or a man hanging on a cross. These affirmations of faith could not be arrived at via 'natural theology'.

THE QUEST FOR THE REASONABLENESS OF CHRISTIANITY

'Natural theology' seeks to demonstrate the 'reasonableness' of Christianity. The greatest example of such an attempt in the history of Christian theology was, perhaps, the 13th-century work of Thomas Aquinas, which created a brilliant synthesis between biblical faith and Aristotelian philosophy.

This has exercised enormous influence on Christian theology ever since. But, as Jesuit theologian Michael Buckley points out, the synthesis was achieved by dividing our knowledge of God into two parts. On the one hand are those things which (it is claimed) can be demonstrated by the use of reason alone—such as the existence of God and the soul. On the other hand are things which cannot be demonstrated by reason but must be accepted in faith—such as the Trinity, the Incarnation and the Atonement.

In making this distinction, Aquinas was departing from an earlier tradition of Christian theology (notably represented in Augustine and Anselm) which has seen faith not as an alternative to reason but as the only pathway to knowledge. 'I believe in order to know,' said Augustine. We learn to speak by trustfully repeating the words we hear our parents speak. We start at school by believing what the teachers and the textbooks tell us. We do not begin to know anything by doubting everything. Faith is not an alternative to knowing; it is the only pathway to knowing.

But Christendom was now committed to the enterprise of certain knowledge, a kind of knowledge which did not depend on faith. The trouble was that uncertainty kept creeping in. The new ideas of people like Galileo and Copernicus upset beliefs which had seemed certain. We always thought that the sun rose in the east and went down in the west. But now apparently it doesn't. It is the earth which is moving. But the earth still feels quite firm. Who can you believe?

It was all very upsetting. Nothing seemed absolutely certain. In this atmosphere of prevailing doubt, a cardinal of the Church spotted a bright young philosopher named René Descartes and gave him a commission to produce an indubitable proof of the existence of God. Descartes carried out the commission by starting from an indubitable certainty ('I think, therefore I am') and building upon it a structure of knowledge by means of deductions having the certainty and clarity of mathematics. Beliefs which could not be validated in terms of this method of proof were to be doubted.

Thus the method of Augustine and Anselm was reversed. The pathway to certain knowledge was to be doubt, not faith. Criticism was to be the acid which would dissolve beliefs which are not certain. It was this that made possible the Enlightenment, with its vision of a world unified by means of a universal reason. It was this vision which inspired the explosive expansion of European power throughout the world in the 19th and early 20th centuries.

But the Enlightenment project is collapsing. Nietzsche saw that the elevation of the critical principle to primacy must end in self-destruction. I can only doubt a proposition on the basis of what I believe to be true. The critical principle eventually destroys itself and—as Nietzsche saw—leaves behind only the will to power. Nietzsche's *Genealogy of Morals* and Foucault's *Archaeology of the Social Sciences* express the fact that the 'eternal truths' of reason are in fact products of particular human histories. They have no over-arching claim to absolute truth.

Here is the contemporary context for our preaching, a disintegrating 'modernity' which believes (or once believed) in the possibility of rationally demonstrable eternal truths, and a rising 'postmodernism' which sees all claims to truth as products of particular cultures and particular histories.

How then do we make our case to an unbelieving world deeply influenced by these trends?

RECOVERING THE STORY

For the thousand-year period which created Europe as a society, the focus of reliable truth was in a story—the cosmic story from creation to consummation, told in the Bible. To accept a *story* as the focus of reliable truth is to walk by faith and not by indubitable certainty, because the story has not yet ended.

In one sense, therefore, the postmodernists are allies. We do not claim to offer indubitable certainties in the style of Descartes. Our whole business is to tell the story of God's mighty acts.

To accept the story as our starting point means precisely that it is a starting point and not a cut-off point. It is the beginning of our exploration, not the end of it. For if Jesus is indeed the incarnation of the Word of God, then it is by taking him as our clue that we shall come to understand the whole of our experience of the world.

It follows that in our preaching we traverse the same ground as that which natural theology invited us to traverse—but in the opposite direction. We take the story as our starting point, and from there we set out to explore.

Of course this starting point can be questioned. As we know, it is doubted by the majority of humankind. But the moment we step outside of the reigning worldview of contemporary Western society we discover that it is also phrased in assumptions which are by no means indubitable. The plain truth is that the whole idea of an indubitable certainty which has a supra-cultural authority, on the basis of which we can judge all human efforts to grasp the truth, is an illusion. What is in fact available to us in the gospel is a life of personal faith in a personal God, a personal commitment to him as he calls us to follow him in the quest for truth, a truth which we shall only know in all its fullness at the end of the journey.

So apologetic preaching has to be biblical preaching. We do not start from something supposed to be more reliable than God's revelation of himself in Jesus. We start from the story of what God has done and seek to show how this enables us to understand the whole of our experience, and not only to understand, but to be reconciled, to be delivered from our alienation and enabled to know that God works all things together for those who love him.

But this will only happen if the preacher is one who is learning through patient discipleship to live in the world of the Bible so that it becomes truly the context in which everything is understood. And that is a lifelong business.

PREACHING AT 'OCCASIONAL' SERVICES

Geoffrey Hunter and Richard Broadberry (1986/1996)

WELCOME OF INFANTS

All traditions have special services to welcome infants into church fellowship, e.g. Baptism, Thanksgiving, Dedication. Preaching at such services, despite the difficulties, should not be avoided. For the preacher, a difficulty is that s/he is not the centre of attention. A difficulty for the congregation is often minimal connection with the church. So its attention may be hard to win, especially if two or more families are involved.

Nowadays welcome of children is increasingly and rightly part of a main service, to which the sermon is normally geared, though from time to time focus on the infants may be desirable. The theology of the service will have been dealt with during the preparation of the families. So the sermon can take one basic idea from the appointed Scriptures, and fix everyone's attention on that. Focus upon the beginnings of growth and upon God's supplies for this within his church. At believer's (adult) baptism, constraints are not as pressing, but as always be brief, simple, and self-effacing. The *shared* faith of congregation and candidates needs to be celebrated.

MARRIAGES

At a wedding, a word of encouragement to the couple, and through them to the congregation, is needed. Use a light touch and do not alienate by tedious length or 'churchy' mannerisms or forced humour. The congregation will have to endure more speeches—some of them embarrassing!—

later at the reception. So set an example of conciseness, relevance and godly help. A theme can be drawn from the Scripture readings, hymns, or even personal characteristics of the couple.

FUNERALS

Frequently the minister is the only person to speak publicly at a funeral. A sermon early in the service can set the tone of the occasion. It is the minister's privilege and obligation to proclaim the good news of Jesus Christ to those who have (maybe temporarily) lost hope.

Always speak of the deceased by name; speak at a measured pace; avoid shouting insensitively. Recall how Jesus ministered to people in emotional turmoil. Acknowledge the support of the congregation: they look to the minister to express thoughts, wishes, tributes and sympathy otherwise unexpressed. In thanksgiving invite them to recall their own personal memories. The community is demeaned, the bereaved hurt and 'the good is oft interred with their bones' if, at a funeral, the preacher does not recall what has been true and good in that person's life. Mention of foibles can bring the consolation of reality and humour. Where there is sin, or failed relationships, the proclamation of Christ's death for our sins can heal in bereavement through repentance and forgiveness. The message of Easter Day proclaims that the Christian hope is in 'the life of the world to come' and in the prayerful fellowship of 'the communion of saints'.

We recognize that the emphasis in some traditions, e.g. the modern Roman Catholic rite, is away from the deceased to the eternal gospel. Nevertheless, the eternal gospel must be related to the here and now: abstract preaching at funerals does not help the congregation.

❀

ANOTHER COUNTRY: PREACHING ON CIVIC OCCASIONS

Michael Henshall

'Fix bayonets. Colour Party—Slow March.' The stentorian command echoed and re-echoed through the great parish church. In the vestry the newly ordained curate had apoplexy. 'Colour Party—Halt.' The Rector received the flags, some still bearing the emblems of conflict. The high altar was draped. The fuming curate, muttering 'outrage, outrage', was ordered to his stall.

It was the first Sunday in July. It was a huge civic occasion. The Battle of the Somme was being recalled with innumerable tears. On this day in July 1916 the Lancashire Regiments lost 5000 men in five minutes, and 20,000 lay dead before the sun set. The wounds of the community were still raw.

In the morning the curate simply saw the contradiction of raw steel before the altar of God. By late afternoon he knew at least something of the raw steel twisting in the lives of loved ones. He came quickly to acknowledge the importance of civic occasions in a deeply hurt community.

The skilful preacher on this emotive day based his sermon on the hymn that had just been sung, 'I vow to thee, my country'. He touched gently on the theme of patriotism and on the significance of sacrifice. But then the tone changed. In the hushed church, filled with a thousand 'live' soldiers and a thousand others with bleeding hearts and terrible memories of a postman with a telegram, he said slowly, 'And there's another country I've heard of long ago'—and then came Christ and the gospel. Now it was the sacrifice of Calvary, not only the sacrifices of the Somme. Loyalty to the Regiment became loyalty to the Lord Jesus. The emblems of suffering on the draped flags became the emblems of Christ on his crucified body. Here was no Billy Graham appeal to come forward. Of direct evangelism there was none. But the sermon spoke volumes to the civic gathering, many, like Simon of Cyrene, compelled to be on parade.

I was present on that day. Subsequently I made extensive use of that same hymn and those two significant words, 'another country'. I have used them for Lord Mayors being churched, for medics and Masons, for the Women's Institute and for the Lifeboat Institution. I believe that one of the great secrets of preaching on civic occasions is to employ a topic that enables an effective, if understated, transition to happen. I describe it as helping people to journey from religion to Christianity or from a mere congregation to a dynamic community. There are many choices to hand, but I have found the use of 'there's another country' a civic winner.

Communication, to be effective, need not be direct. Sophisticated evangelism and civic services initially seem poles apart. Superficially they are; spiritually they are not. Neither troops of Scouts nor serried ranks of the WI take kindly to 'Are you saved?' or 'Do you love the Lord?' Both questions matter eternally, but they are capable of translation into simple, subtle language chiselled for the particular congregation.

In Western society, even residual Christian faith is in retreat, but hints and guesses of a bygone glory linger and lurk in the corporate un-conscious. Herein still lies a major gospel opportunity. Herein lies the raison d'être of the civic service. After all, the Christian gospel, when first preached, was clearly for Tommies in khaki, for Masons in Lodges, for mayors in chains of office, for women in unions or institutes, for carollers at Christmas—in fact, for everyone.

❦

SUFFERING AND SILENCE

Rod Garner (1997)

At the foot of the Mount of Olives stands one of Jerusalem's most beautiful churches, the Church of Gethsemane. I am always moved by the atmosphere: the dim light filtering through the purple windows; the pervasiveness of prayer and the magnificent mosaic showing Christ offering his suffering to the Father. As 16 countries contributed to its construction, the building is also called the Church of All Nations. Their languages are everywhere to be heard in the vicinity of Gethsemane but only silence fills the interior of the church. Perhaps it has something to do with the notice that reads, 'No Religious Explanations Here'. For a while interpreters and guides fall silent and pilgrims are left to form their own conclusions concerning the mysteries of Christ's Passion.

Holy Week is the time of year when the preacher feels compelled to proffer religious explanations. Suffering is a taxing subject at any time but never more so than when we follow Christ from Gethsemane to Golgotha. Talks and meditations are laboured over, so that our listeners might enter more fully into the agony of the 'strange man on the cross'. Sermons struggle with the necessity of Calvary as we seek to give fresh meanings to old truths. Even if this death was like no other death, how, precisely, does it afford us salvation without offending our moral sensibilities? We sense that we have a duty to speak, but we are also (or should be) deeply conscious of the limits of our language as it confronts the tragedy of divine love and the extremity of human wickedness. Talk can be cheap in Holy Week; clichés so easily miss the mark and stones have never been a substitute for bread.

'No Religious Explanations Here.' I confess that I missed the notice on my first visit to Gethsemane. It was brought to my attention by a Church of Scotland minister speaking on the radio the morning after the massacre of the innocents at Dunblane. His measured words obeyed the injunction: he would not trivialize children's savage deaths with inept discourse nor would he seek to make religious capital out of such awful calamity. Explanation was of no use here. He offered listeners the way of silence as the only entry into a community that was immersed in its own Gethsemane.

There are scriptural precedents for this advice. The writer of Ecclesiastes reminds us that 'there is a time for speech and a time for silence' (3:7). We might also recall that when the friends of Job came to him in his anguish, seven days and nights passed before they spoke a word, 'for they saw that his suffering was very great' (Job 2:13). In our own time, as Jewish thinkers surveyed the aftermath of the Holocaust, some insisted that the only possible stance in the light of such wickedness was that of silence. A text hallowed by Jewish tradition is: 'And Aaron was silent' (Leviticus 10:3). Holy Week does not have to be immersed in a torrent of religious words—savaged by E.M. Forster as 'poor little talkative Christianity'. The anguish of Jesus and the awful ambivalence precipitated in people's lives by his message requires us to be reticent rather than dumb—employing words in such a way that the pathos of the Passion is not, unwittingly, rendered facile by a misconceived desire to explain.

Preachers need to be poets as Good Friday approaches—spare with their allusions, deft with the language they employ in the service of a gospel indelibly marked by paradox as well as grief. This is not a time to convert the gospel into explicit and unequivocal assertions but rather to take seriously the wisdom of W.H. Auden when he writes:

> *Truth in any serious sense*
> *Like Orthodoxy, is a reticence.*
> SHIELD OF ACHILLES, 46

If we owe this to Christ, then no less do we also have a duty to our listeners, those faithful ones who bring their aspirations and ravaged lives to our churches to be touched by God. They too have become acquainted with the holy ground of pain and are moved by the memory of one who is nailed upon the cross and mocked. The 'old, old story' is both terrible and familiar, with a potency all of its own. Our integrity as preachers, and the pastoral needs of our people, require that our words at such times should be well chosen; where possible, few; and unashamedly elusive. 'No Religious Explanations Here.' It has the makings of a text.

❦

PREACHING IN TIMES OF CRISIS

Paul Johns (2002, updated)

Since 11 September 2001, I've felt more than usually out of my depth as a preacher. Should I stick safely to the set agenda, in faith that a lectionary-guided missile will always hit some target somewhere? Or should I be prepared to boldly go, Bible in hand, into the unknown of the crisis itself in faith that God will answer me out of the whirlwind?

Public crises have many faces—political, military and economic; and they throw up plenty of human interest stories. The media spin them all before our eyes. But for us preachers the reported crisis is at heart a crisis in the relationship between God and his creation; a crisis in the life of God himself. I feel I must try, however clumsily, to probe beneath the surface of the crisis that broke on 11 September, to get at its hidden inside. Crisis preaching involves declaring what is going on behind what is manifestly happening—which is what the first Christians did when they recounted the story of the crucifixion of Jesus.

This doesn't mean that our preaching must be news-driven. The media don't decide crises. In one important sense, the relationship between God and his creation is always in crisis. God provokes crises as he persistently confronts us with our redemption; and God's crisis should run like a golden thread through all preaching.

But we shouldn't let that lead us to treat each particular crisis as just one more piece of evidence of our continuing need of salvation, so that our every sermon steers the congregation to the same general conclusion by way of different convenient topical illustrations. Particular crises—like 11 September—are important in their own right.

Crises hurt and kill. Crises cause grief and anger. They make people resentful, fearful; they pitch us into emergency and uncertainty. Crises make us wonder. With each crisis people ask, 'How did this come about?' and look back for answers. Then they look forward and ask, 'What should be done to stop this happening again?' In other words we set the present crisis in the context of past and future; and begin to imagine it as the defining moment, the turning point in a narrative.

Furthermore, it is through particular crises, rather than in general terms, that God characteristically speaks and acts—through the crisis of liberation for a slave nation; the crisis of exile for a degenerate nation; and, definitively, through the crisis of a crucifixion in front of the same nation oppressed and boiling with resentment and expectation. God does not keep on saying the same old things in different ways. With each crisis he writes a new chapter in his story, tells us something new.

Certainly, St Paul drew transcendent conclusions from the particular crisis of the crucifixion; but only because he had first been caught up in that particular crisis and, as it were, discovered it from the inside. His discovery made him reinterpret the past and imagine the future anew. Preaching has to repeatedly rediscover that crucifixion crisis and re-imagine its significance in all other crises.

So each crisis is unique, for God as well as for us. God spoke, speaks, will speak specifically and contemporaneously. So let's preach our way through each crisis very seriously as an event in which God is saying something new. We don't have to distil the whole word of God from each crisis. God has not packed all he has to say into 11 September. The meaning of each crisis is always incomplete. For there are always more crises, more God-words, to come.

Each crisis attracts all sorts of explanations and proposals for action, offered by all sorts of authority figures and experts. Some try to be detached and objective; some extrude conclusions out of their favourite dogmas; and others simply pass judgment on those who have done this or offer advice to those who need to do that. We need to listen, sift, digest and avoid regurgitation. For we are offered our distinctive way of entering and interpreting the crisis.

To preach in crisis is to discover and declare that two things converge. First, our almost instinctive wish to find meaning and security in a crisis by seeking answers to the questions 'How has it come about?' and 'How do we now plot a better future?': that is, to create a narrative context for the crisis. Second, our biblical understanding of God who is telling his story; who speaks anew now as of old, and will speak again and again in days to come.

To preach in crisis is to invite the congregation to witness a meeting between today's events and biblical text so that events and text illuminate each other. The Bible has things to say about where, according to God's story, we have come from and where we are going. Through contemporary events, discerned in the light of the Bible, God tells us where, in his story, we are now.

There is a need for not just one meeting between Bible and present crisis, but many. The Bible has many relevant things to say; the current crisis has many sides to it. There is no one biblical 'answer' to the crisis. There is room and need for plenty of sermons. Here, for example, are three pairings of event and text, which have set my imagination going, and served my preaching.

INNOCENT VICTIMS?

America was without question a victim on 11 September. Thousands of innocent Americans suffered. Soon after, some commentators began to argue that to be a victim is one thing, to be innocent is another; that 'America' had somehow helped to bring this disaster on itself; that America needed to learn lessons for the future. In the book of Job, suffering apparently innocent, arguably merited, leads a seemingly impregnable man into a period of agonizing reflection on his past, and into a future based on a new understanding of God.

HOLY WAR?

11 September has made an issue of 'jihad' understood as holy all-out war. Osama bin Laden called for jihad against America to purify tainted Islam. President Bush called for a global war against terrorism, to protect God-blessed America. This clash between jihad by terror and jihad by B52 seems to offer no future, no better world, beyond conclusive defeat of the enemy.

Saul was a fundamentalist committed to 'jihad' against early Christians. Saul became Paul. Gifted with a new worldview, he shared (read Ephesians) a vision of a new community in which the division of the world into 'holy' and 'infidel' is removed. The case for militant jihad falls. The real jihad for the future is against 'principalities and powers'—dark destructive forces of moral corruption which dehumanize us; and for Christians this jihad is in principle already won in Christ.

The USA and its allies have now overthrown Saddam Hussein in the second Gulf War of 2003. The risk was considerable; the outcome remains uncertain. The story of David, Nabal and Abigail (1 Samuel 25) tells how good leadership often demands restraint rather than resort to superior force. It tells how costly it is to be a peacemaker trying to save powerful and obdurate enemies from their worst selves, and to protect innocent people from suffering. But the peacemaker wins the day; and David, who militarily has the upper hand, does exercise restraint and thus shows himself fit to be a future king.

None of these examples claims to be either a conclusive comment on the event, or authoritative exegesis of the text. They are rather attempts to invite the congregation to imagine one situation (the present event) in terms of another (the biblical text); and so to open windows on to fresh and distinctive Christian ways of seeing into the crisis.

Imagination is one of God's greatest and most neglected gifts—never more needed than in time of crisis, when we tend to take refuge in familiar ways of looking at things only to find that the wine bursts the skins. Imaginative preaching treats people and events as symbolic; uses language metaphorically, poetically; is exploratory, suggestive, and envisioning.

The use of imagination is based on the conviction that the Christian faith is founded upon one huge and developed imaginative insight into the crisis of the cross and resurrection of Jesus. Imagination is the gift most needed by the preacher who yearns to expose what is going on beneath the surface of the crisis; to set it in the context of God's past and God's future; and so help the worshipping community to discover how to live and what to say today.

INTRODUCTION

Stephen Wright

This final part of the book focuses on the human beings involved in the encounter of preaching, and the all-important relationship between them which enables it to work.

If the last two articles in Part 1 suggested the excitement and risk involved in preaching as a human venture, the first two in this part, by David Day and Lavinia Byrne, suggest the discipline and self-examination necessary. If the preachers are to be God's mouthpiece, they must know themselves and the particular temptations that attend them both as individuals and as preachers.

The next two articles bring into focus the listeners, indispensable partners in the preaching enterprise. Eric Devenport highlights the value of a preacher's having an ongoing pastoral relationship with a congregation. Peter Kerr discusses some specific things for which a preacher should 'listen' in their congregation—stages of faith, personality, and congregational self-image.

One of these dimensions, personality, is then taken up in more detail by Angela Butler, showing the importance of knowing one's own preferences and being aware of the diversity of others'. A further key factor is gender, discussed by Jane Craske.

How, finally, should listeners evaluate the preaching that they hear? This is not a matter of subjecting preachers to grillings over Sunday roast (whether in their presence or their absence!), but of encouraging their ongoing growth and development. Finding appropriate mechanisms for feedback is vital, as Gethin Thomas shows, and John James offers some wise criteria to use.

THE LENTEN PREACHER

David Day (1999)

My subject is the Lent which the preacher must carry about in the heart,
not the content of what a preacher ought to say during Lent. A traditional
focus in Lent has been the temptations of Jesus. Since the Gospel
narrative is about Jesus' awareness that he is the Son of God, I want to
explore the idea of the preacher as one who stands in the presence of
God, is called to speak in the name of God, and to be God's mouthpiece.
The voice of the tempter which as a preacher I must learn to recognize is
the voice that says, 'If you really are the herald, the messenger, the
mouthpiece of God, then...'

STONES INTO BREAD

The first temptation is about *the source of my life* as a preacher. It presses
the question, 'Where do I go for sustenance?' and therefore, 'Where do I
go for the source of my sermons?' The temptation is to seek food in the
wrong place.

Dressed in borrowed clothes

The temptation might appear first in a desperate desire to rush to the
commentaries, sermon outlines, joke books or other people's sermons
(an abomination to the Lord) as opposed to listening in silence and
being prepared patiently to wait for God to speak. Fred Craddock gives
sound advice: 'Never begin with the commentaries. They suppress and
intimidate the preacher. After all, who is going to venture a thought or an
interpretation when at the very same desk are six internationally known
Bible scholars?' (*Preaching*, Abingdon Press, p. 106).

The fast-food sermon

A second way in which this temptation shows itself is in seizing upon an idea and preaching on that rather than working hard at what the text really says. It is tempting to use Mark's account of Jesus and the leper in Mark 1:40–45 as an excuse to parade some interesting thoughts about Jesus' healing ministry and ours. But the distinctive thrust of the text is then lost, swallowed up in generalities. There is much more in this passage than an opportunity to discuss my views on healing. Most of us could knock up a passable sermon on the prodigal son. We let the words escape from the mouth without having engaged the brain. A mere glance at the Call of Isaiah will provoke a pop-up sermon on the Vision of God, Sense of Sin, Forgiveness and the Call to Witness.

But the feel of the passage is something else, and a more patient reading will pick up the terror, the pain and the burden of the prophet's experience. The hymn says, 'Bright the vision that delighted once the sight of Judah's seer.' I question if the man who wrote that had ever read Isaiah's call.

These are ways of stuffing ourselves full of fast-food sermons rather than turning faithfully to the source of our life. Listening in silence is an act of trust in the love of God and his call to me to preach his word for this occasion. It requires me to believe that he will not betray me. He will feed me. I don't have to force stones into bread, even on a Saturday evening.

Shuffling the cards

Sermons cannot be detached from the people who preach them. Where is the source of my life when I am not being a preacher? When my sermon does not reflect my life, the congregation will often sense that sermon and self are not quite in tune. I may be trying to drink from a well that is running dry. Where should I go when I want a life-giving word to preach? To the life-giver.

Unfortunately, it is easy to do no more in the pulpit than shuffle a well-worn pack of cards, laying them out in different sequences and arranging them in pretty patterns. Resisting this temptation calls for reality in the pulpit. Sermons are real when there is genuine engagement with the problems of life, when the preacher speaks out of his or her own experience of God and the struggles of the life of faith, without disparaging either. One preacher said that the finest compliment he had ever received was from someone who said, 'You cut the crap.' When the sermon touches reality, when it deals with deeply felt emotions and when it opens up the spiritual dimension of our existence, then people not only get the sense that God is real for the preacher but also that he is real for them and is speaking to them.

These three examples illustrate the truth that the preacher lives not by bread but by the living word which comes from God's mouth. If we fall victim to the temptation to settle for anything less, then the first casualty is our *authenticity*.

THE PINNACLE OF THE TEMPLE

The pinnacle of the temple is about *the nature of my relationship with God*. In the desert Israel asked, 'Is the Lord among us or not?' with the underlying complaint, 'We don't think he is. Let us violently test the relationship.' From this act of rebellion arose the complaints and the ungrateful murmurings which came to be called 'The day of provocation'. Israel's behaviour was essentially manipulative. It was an attempt to force God's hand.

For Jesus, the temptation exposes the difference between jumping as a way of trusting God and jumping as a way of provoking him. To the casual observer there is no visible difference between the two. Jumping from the pinnacle might be an instance of trusting God but might be provoking him. And no one outside your head will ever know; only you and God will know the inside story.

From inside the relationship, of course, trusting God has a different feel about it. It involves waiting on him, being summoned, and obeying in some fear and reluctance. There is all the difference in the world between being brought by God to the pinnacle and called in the name of scripture to risk leaping into the abyss in blind trust—and jumping in order to force him to bend to your desires.

As a preacher, I find it easy to take God for granted and use him for my purposes. He will come when I snap my fingers. He is a slot-machine God. I am not humbly standing beneath the word or at the foot of the cross but proudly calculating and independent. I am six feet above contradiction. This is a long way to fall, but I'm not bothered, because he will catch me and bail me out.

At the heart of the temptation lies the question, 'Will I treat God as truly my friend, my intimate? Or do I use him and abuse his commitment to me?' Calvin said, dauntingly, 'Voilà the pulpit, the throne of God.' We stand in the holy place and yet know that it is possible to abuse the relationship. The first casualty then is love and intimacy. The friendship is damaged when we take it for granted. What might be the homiletical examples?

Back of an envelope

A minister told his congregation, 'What I'm to say to you this morning God only knows.' They were not impressed with this casual sauntering up to the pulpit. It represented a lack of care, a dereliction of duty, a failure to listen and pray.

Presuming on God, taking him for granted in this way, is very different from the cry of Moses: 'If your presence does not go with us, do not send us up from here' (Exodus 33:15). This is the cry of the man to whom God would speak face to face, 'as a man speaks with his friend'. This is the man who came away from God's presence with his face shining. Unfortunately, the shining face cannot be kept in a jar by the door. It comes from fasting and waiting, looking and listening. Back-of-an-envelope sermons, ill-prepared and casually thrown together, betray the friendship. The wonder of it all is that very often, in his grace God catches us, even when we don't deserve it.

Pulpit performance

Though clearly preaching is a craft, a cunningly devised piece of persuasion, which aims to produce an effect, it is still possible to become rather too good at it. Then we can perform superbly and at the same time prostitute our calling. We end up doing it just because we're good at it. Lancelot Andrewes, aware of the peril, prayed, 'Lord, inform my gestures.' Preaching can never be just a performance—at least, not without the loss of something irreplaceable.

Preaching by numbers

The mechanically constructed sermon will not work. An illustration goes in here; here I shout loudly because the argument is weak; I need a joke at the beginning, relevant or not doesn't matter; I tell this anecdote as if it happened to me even when I know it didn't; this sentimental story will move the hearers; I shall not pursue this aspect of the text or this facet of Christian experience because they are messy and complex but I shall move swiftly on to safer ground. Inside your head you know how empty the sermon is.

Convinced by one's own dogma

One of the great expository preachers of the post-war period told a meeting of ministers towards the end of his career: 'If I had my time again I would say what it is really like.' It is possible to preach a message which carries you away by its own rhetoric. There is a proper tension between the great affirmations of the faith, which do take your breath away, and the need to say what it is really like, refusing to distort reality in the interests of an ideology. Life is often more grey and less black-and-white than our preaching suggests.

The ego-trip

Craddock notes the tendency of preachers to gravitate 'towards the best seats in the text'. We need to guard against this possibility. 'If this step is not taken deliberately, it is very likely that the sermon will be prepared and delivered from the choice places in the texts. The congregation will hear loud and clear what is not stated but implied: today our preacher is Paul and we are the Corinthians, today our preacher is the loving father and we are the older son pouting on the back porch' (*Preaching*, Abingdon Press, p. 120).

Richard Lischer identifies 'preaching out of need-love' as another way of feeding up self-esteem: 'Those who preach out of need-love never get enough of preaching. Why? Because they can never get enough of stroking that denies or temporarily controls those terrifying aspects of the self that have not yet been recognized or transcended in Christ. This exaggerated need for self-affirmation turns preaching into therapy—not for the congregation but for the preacher' (*A Theology of Preaching*, Labyrinth, p. 68).

All this from the pulpit, out of the Scriptures and in the name of God. The observer may never suspect that anything is wrong, but we know that somewhere along the way something infinitely precious, *our intimacy with God*, has been put under strain.

THE KINGDOMS OF THE WORLD

The final temptation is about *the focus and direction of my gaze*. In the desert Israel is warned that, once they enter the land, they will be tempted to serve other gods. For Christ the panoramic vision of all the kingdoms of the world represents authority, success and infinite possibility, but only at a price: compromise.

The preacher undergoes a similar temptation: to shape what I have to say by reference not to God but to other voices and other lords. It is easy, for example, to preach a 'smooth' word, which offends no one and reinforces what people want to hear. The smooth word sounds like the gospel, but in fact represents an accommodation to the power and authority of the congregation.

Reframing the truth

Marsha Witten's book, *All is forgiven: the Secular Message of American Protestantism* (Princeton) gives numerous examples of how congregations shape the preacher's preaching. Under the impulse of a variety of rhetorical devices the concept of sin is attenuated; it is deflected away from the listening audience and projected on to specific groups of outsiders. The instances of sin used in sermons carry the message that other people are the ones who sin, whether they are children, adolescents in rebellion, or members of a diseased secular world, caught up in drug abuse, alcoholism, compulsive gambling, murder and prostitution. Sometimes sin is reframed with reference to a social science perspective. Sin is a flaw in a family system, or naiveté, or immaturity. Witten argues that many preachers are engaged in a process of making their message palatable to their listeners.

Properly insulated prophecy

A traditional Ash Wednesday reading from Isaiah 58 calls the preacher to proclaim justice. This theme is a particularly slippery one. It is easy to preach 'prophetically' but run no risk at all of being driven from the building and taken to the brow of a hill by an angry mob.

The most common move is to discourse on safe topics: disarmament, conservation, Third World debt, industrial peace, ethical investment. In the recent past, South Africa and apartheid used to be a popular evil against which to inveigh. There is no chance of being misunderstood or attacked. You might as well preach against marrying your wife's father's mother.

Much the same result is obtained by keeping the treatment general and safe. After all, we might think, ethical and justice issues are so complex. But then, the sermon might as well be taken from the broadsheets or *Frost on Sunday*. The mark of the word that is difficult but necessary, dangerous yet needing to be said, is often its specificity. When the preacher deals with specific and local issues he or she runs the risk of offending the listeners. Amos's remarks about 'cows of Bashan' went down badly with the women of Bashan, however much others enjoyed them. Often general comments are the refuge of the scoundrel or the coward.

None of this is to be understood as a licence for being bad-tempered in the pulpit, of course, but it does remind us how difficult it is to keep our eyes fixed on God when we prepare a sermon and how quickly *integrity* disappears under the cold scrutiny of a disapproving congregation.

These dire warnings may imply an unnecessarily bleak view of the preacher and the preacher's task. That is not their intention. The Lenten themes offer preachers wonderful opportunities to castigate congregations and give full rein to personal prejudices and private niggles. There is no better way to settle old scores. So concentrating on the Lent that the preacher carries around inside is a necessary corrective. It is the homiletical equivalent of Jesus' story about the mote and the beam.

❀

THE ASCETICISM
OF THE PREACHER

Lavinia Byrne (1996)

What is the appropriate asceticism of the preacher? What are the disciplines we should follow? I suggest we ask ourselves four questions.

WHICH IS MY PREFERRED CHRISTIAN MYSTERY?

Is our own private devotion most fed by creation, or incarnation, or redemption? If we do not know our own answer to this, we will be driven by our preference instead of using it to the greater glory of God.

Creation, incarnation and redemption form a triptych and are incomplete without each other. We can visualize a threefold icon, with a central panel and folding flaps with two further panels on them. So too with what I call our theological landscape. One image or one mystery may occupy the central panel, but it is worth remembering the side panels without which the whole is incomplete. If you constantly preach about green concerns without reference to the incarnation and redemption, you will be a sounding gong. If you constantly preach about justice and peace without reference to creation and to the redemption, you will be a crashing cymbal. If you draw crowds to the wounded side of the Saviour without allowing them to marvel at the dawn or kneel at the crib, then you are an empty vessel. Whether open or folded, the three panels of the triptych are in constant conversation with one another, and our task is to eavesdrop, to share the dialogue.

'Pray more' is a totally inadequate prescription for a preacher's discipline, whereas 'know your theological landscape' is a highly significant one. Once we accept that we have theological preferences, we will be able to recognize that we are also highly selective in our reading of the

Scriptures. That is why I believe it is important to work to a lectionary and not simply to choose our own texts. We are forced to grapple with the demands of unfamiliar texts, to make connections which ensure that what we say is vital rather than trite, focused rather than rambly.

WHAT DO I MOST BELIEVE AND WANT
TO TELL PEOPLE ABOUT?

I believe I am a less toxic preacher than I might otherwise be because I have a clear answer to that question. At root, I want to say something deeply simple: 'God loves you.' I heard a priest ask some Sunday school children: 'What were the words which came from God when Jesus stepped out of the water?' A child stepped forward. 'You are my beloved daughter,' she said, 'and I love you very much.' That child had heard the good news preached to her.

WHY DO YOU PREACH?

A third question is 'Why do you preach?' One answer may be because I have to, week after week, and it kills me. Your asceticism is ready made! Just be aware that some of your desperation may creep across into what you are saying. Renewal is a legitimate requirement.

You may be a happy preacher though—and so the question is even more important. Why do you preach? Do you like the sound of your own voice? Is that a bad thing? Mrs Booth must have liked the sound of hers. She could fill a large hall without the use of a microphone. She knew of the power of the human voice to comfort the vacillating and call sinners to the throne of glory. And so I bet she never told that further joke because the first one had worked well; I bet she knew better than to play to the gallery; I bet she didn't ramble, leaning forward cosily for a little unscripted chat—and call that a sermon.

We do not preach because we feel like it, or because we don't feel like it. We preach in order to persuade. We do not preach in order to judge, but in order to illumine.

We are to preach as *listening* people, in several different modes. As pastoral people above all: that means engaging with reality, actually looking it in the face. It means remembering that we preach to people who are like us and not unlike us, intelligent, able, busy, confused, clear-headed, worthy, unworthy human beings. It means remembering that we have to wrestle with the agnosticism and atheism of our times because we seek to give an account of faith in an unbelieving and not a believing world. And we listen as praying, thinking, believing people.

And that is where the crunch really comes. Because in faith we know that the encounter with God always begins in grace. The work of preaching can only safely be undertaken by someone who is grounded in the love of God. Otherwise it becomes your own thing, rather than the thing of God made known in the company of the faithful. Jeremiah knew about this: 'If I say, "I will not mention him, or speak any more in his name", then within me there is something like a burning fire shut up in my bones; I am weary with holding it in, and I cannot' (Jeremiah 20:9).

PREACHING AND PASTORAL RELATIONSHIP

Eric Devenport (1986)

Preaching and pastoral work go hand in hand. This is one of those truths that has to be proclaimed time after time after time, for unless it is heard, then most preaching will not only be dull, but dead.

When we begin a sermon we must start where our hearers are. Start where you think the hearers are, or start where you choose, and the task of getting to them becomes almost impossible after that. Yet if we can start with something that shows that we are with them, rather than standing on high and never really making contact, then eyes look up and almost say to the preacher, 'We're listening. Our eyes are open, show us the Christ, and surely we shall see.'

The best way of knowing where our hearers are, and therefore the point from which we can declare that which we know, is to be in continuing pastoral contact with those to whom we preach. Indeed, the best sermons often grow out of such pastoral contact. We may pick up some question that is being asked directly. Or we realize that some point has been made indirectly on a pastoral visit, which gives us a lead into a sermon. Or perhaps the sermon springs out of a Bible study group where we've heard our fellow Christians speak the truth in love, and really express, in their own terms, what a particular passage has meant to them. Or perhaps the same group has prepared a sermon together, and not only the local illustrations, but the deep insights, have come from a shared knowledge of the place in which they live, and the people among whom they live and work.

However the pastoral contact takes place, we know how vital it is. Every preacher also knows the effect of trying to preach when we have not got that sort of pastoral background. We preached a sermon at home, and we could feel that it worked. Yet a week or two later we were asked to preach in a neighbouring church, and decided to preach the same sermon. Here it was like preaching against a brick wall.

Preaching is never done in a vacuum. It is proclaiming God to living men and women. Preaching, therefore, calls for knowledge of people and of the contemporary world and social situation in which we preach.

What then of the peripatetic preacher, the bishop and others who go from place to place, and never appear in the same pulpit on two Sundays in succession? The cynical would say, of course, that maybe that is why most bishops cannot preach, because they don't have enough contact with 'real' people. Others, a little kinder, would declare that because they're called upon to stand in a pulpit too often, they cannot be expected to prepare properly. Both these things can sadly be true. Yet surely the idea that preaching and pastoral work go hand in hand is true for the peripatetic preacher as well as for any other. It may be more difficult to start where the listeners are, but it is still vital to have some sort of pastoral background or the preaching will, indeed, be done in a vacuum.

Perhaps the pastoral contact will be through the local minister. Listening to him or her will open up the way of communication. Perhaps there will be some knowledge of the particular church and its difficulties or needs. Perhaps there will even be something about the church building which can provide a way in.

Some of us are inevitably peripatetic preachers. Yet nothing can take the place of the regular preaching of one who knows the people and who preaches to and in their situation, and shows forth Christ in that place. Where there is such a person it will be especially true that the congregation will have learned to expect something of the preacher—a well-prepared, well-planned diet which they can digest, and which will build them up in the body of Christ. They will know that these are not just a few random thoughts on a week's news, or even a New Testament lecture, half digested in the first place and now half forgotten. These will be for them the words of life, coming not only out of the life which they know, and speaking to it, but coming also out of the Word which is life, and being alive because of that.

'WHAT ARE YOU HEARING AT THE BACK?' LISTENING TO THE LISTENERS

Peter Kerr (1997)

It is an experience common to most preachers, and one that can take even the most experienced by surprise: a member of the congregation after the service comments on just how much a particular point was appreciated. The preacher tries not to look puzzled or embarrassed, for what the listener in the congregation had 'heard' was certainly not part of the preacher's intention, nor to be construed from the actual word spoken!

'Nothing was further from my mind!' the preacher exclaims—inwardly. And yet it should be no surprise, for just as the teacher has to come to terms with the fact that what the student learns is distinct and sometimes tenuously related to what the teacher thinks he or she has taught, so the preacher needs to realize that what is heard by the congregation will sometimes bear little similarity to what was so carefully prepared in the study. It may be an unwelcome and frustrating observation, but what is heard is not always what is preached, especially if the preacher, in preparation, only pays attention to their own preaching and not to the congregation's listening. To preach effectively is to be a sensitive and conscientious listener, as well as a theologically articulate and meticulously prepared minister of the word.

The argument of this article is that just as in the final analysis what is learned is more important than what is taught, so what is heard is more important than what is prepared or preached. The congregation will only hear the words of a preacher who pays attention to the congregation and understands who they are both as individuals and as a group.

If preaching is a corporate event involving both preacher and listener opening themselves to the presence of the Spirit, then surely it is crucial that some attempt be made to understand the listening of the congregation. What can be said about the congregation as listeners and therefore as participants in the preaching process? There are several factors that should be taken into account.

STAGES OF FAITH

The first is the recognition and appreciation that within any congregation, different people will be at a variety of different stages in their 'faith journey'. Some are at the 'milk' stage, some are looking for 'solid food' (1 Corinthians 3:2; Hebrews 5:12).

Much thought has been given to understanding the stages of religious development (see James Fowler, *Stages in Religious Development*, Harper & Row; *Becoming Adult, Becoming Christian*, Harper & Row; Jeff Astley, *How Faith Grows*, Church House Publishing; John Hull, *What Prevents Christian Adults Learning*, SCM Press). An early pioneer in this field was Friedrich Von Hugel (*The Mystical Element in Religion*, Dent). He proposes three main elements in our religious experience: the institutional, the critical, and the mystical, corresponding to the three main stages in human development—infancy, adolescence and adulthood.

Infancy is characterized by an attitude of acceptance. Infants accept as true what authority figures—parents, teachers or clergy—tell them. Truth for them resides in the institution—family, school or church. Answers are expected and given.

Adolescence is the age of questioning when the critical element in religion is dominant. Nothing is sacrosanct. Everything has to be tested. Institutional conventions, previously happily received, must now be vigorously dismantled and examined under the intellectual microscope. It is the stage when we seek what Fowler calls an 'autonomous' faith.

In adulthood, we become aware of our inner world, its complexity and incommunicability. We live with ambiguity and paradox. We are sometimes confused, sometimes fascinated, sometimes in awe at the deep mystery of our being and of Being itself. We become aware of the mystical element in religion. It is called the 'conjunctive' stage by Fowler, the stage when we begin to 'get it together' in the sense that we begin to appreciate the desirability of all the elements, institutional, critical and mystical.

The problem for the preacher is not just that the congregation will contain people at different stages, but that the stages are not necessarily successive and that, in each adult, including the preacher, all the elements —institutional, critical and mystical—will to a greater or lesser extent be present. Effective preachers, therefore, must first acknowledge to themselves which stage predominates in their own lives at a particular time (and this may require help) and then vary the style and content of preaching so that over a period it will appeal to people at the different stages of development.

PERSONALITY TYPE

The congregation's listening may also be affected by the personality type of the various individuals in the congregation. The Myers-Briggs Type Indicator® is a well-tried psychometric test now widely used both in business and the church to indicate how individuals prefer to think and operate in the world, the areas in which they are particularly gifted, and other aspects which are less well developed (see Roy Oswald and Otto Kroeger, *Personality and Religious Leadership*, Alban Institute; David Keirsey and Marilyn Briggs, *Please Understand Me*, Gnosology Books).

One of the more obvious preferences revealed by the questionnaire is that for extraversion or introversion—whether a person is energized and refreshed by contact with others, or by being alone. Both types enjoy preaching, not just the extraverts! However, introvert preachers tend to be less in touch with the impact of their words and so may be less aware of the congregation's listening than the extravert. They may come over as being rather cryptic since they often say too little for fear of repeating themselves. Extravert preachers, on the other hand, may hammer a point to death. Perhaps more relevant to the subject in hand are two of the other pairs of preferences: sensing and intuition, and thinking and feeling.

Sensing types prefer dealing with facts and realities that can be observed through the five senses, whereas intuitive types are interested in making sense and meaning, seeing possibilities and making connections. It is reckoned that there is a higher percentage of intuitives among the clergy than among the general population, so the chances are that an intuitive (and often introverted) minister will be preaching to a sensing (and often extravert) congregation.

The other pair of preferences, thinking and feeling, have a similar potential for mismatch between preacher and listening congregation. Those with a thinking preference like a well-argued logical approach to preaching. They prefer to be won over by force of argument. The 'feelers', however, are more interested in relationships and experience.

This type of analysis suggests at least two tasks to preachers who are concerned about the effective listening of the congregation. First they must be aware of their own preferences; second, they must compose sermons which accommodate the different types of personality amongst the listeners.

CONGREGATIONAL IDENTITY

Another factor of relatively recent interest and research that will influence how preachers are received is their appreciation of the congregation's identity or self-image (see Neville Clark, *Preaching in Context*, Kevin Mayhew; C. Dudley & S. Johnson, *Energising the Congregation*, Westminster John Knox Press; James F. Hopewell, *Congregation Stories and Structures*, SCM Press; Leonora Tubbs Tisdale, *Preaching as Local Theology and Folk Art*, Fortress Press).

The corporate identity of a church will be shaped by various influences: the past, its heroes, memories and traditions, the community in which it is set, the building and its physical location. It will be expressed in the stories people tell, in the way things are done, and in how people talk of themselves as a church. These descriptions are sometimes given scriptural warranty. A church may consider itself a family because it considers that intimacy and personal relationships should have a high priority. Another church would use the more businesslike and impersonal terms, 'congregation' or 'household of faith'. In a town with several churches, one may consider itself to be 'the parish church', whereas a small group of worshippers in a rural hamlet may talk of themselves as just a faithful remnant. Congregations may identify themselves as 'Catholic' or 'Spirit-filled' or 'Low church' (though interestingly, the latter term is not often used as a self-designation).

Whatever the self-image of a group of worshippers, they will switch off if they sense that the preacher is not aware of that self-image. This is not to argue that the preacher should not work to change the self-image of the congregation. If the purpose of preaching is the formation and re-formation of the people of God, then it may be a priority. However, whether this is a priority or not, effective preaching will always depend on informed engagement with the congregation's self-identity.

GENDER

Congregational identity may also dictate ('we are a traditional con-gregation') that people listen differently to women preachers than to men. In a pioneering book (*Wrestling with the Patriarchs: Issues for Women Preachers*, Abingdon Press), Lee McGhee of Yale Divinity School explores how congregations perceive and listen to women preaching.

Obviously the sometimes entrenched and suspicious attitudes of a traditionally male institution can conspire to deafen the ear to the female voice in the pulpit. However, McGhee suggests that women themselves, because of their own learned behaviour, may also contribute to the muff-ling of their own authentic theological voice being heard in preaching. Drawing on the work of Carol Gilligan (*In a Different Voice: Psychological Theory and Women's Development*, Harvard) on how women make moral decisions, McGhee argues that sensitivity to relationships plays a crucial part in the way women come to moral decisions, in contrast to men who tend to focus more on principles and moral dictates. The same applies in preaching. The big issue for women is how to give voice to what they know in the pulpit without threatening the relationships with their listeners whose affirmation and support they value. For women, more than for men, there is a real conflict between the claims of relation-ality and of truth, between their experience of God's Word and their relationships with others. So McGhee concludes:

In preaching, more than any other form of public address or communication...
a woman feels called to express what she knows. Yet, in the very process of
preaching—of 'giving voice' to what she sees and knows—a woman risks her
relationship to God, her relationship to self and her relationship to others...
Women preachers tell me 'I have to say this because this is the truth as I know
it, but I feel the tension. I wonder "what is the Word of God here?" Do I dare
it?' (p. 48)

The question of whether this need to defer to the listening congregation is an exclusively female trait or one that is characteristic of a certain type of personality, male and female, is not addressed by McGhee. The Myers-Briggs Type Indicator ® referred to earlier would suggest that what is being discussed here is the difference between Thinking (principle/reason-focused) and Feeling (relationship-focused) types. But the general point still holds, that the congregation may not hear the truth of God as revealed to the preacher (male or female) because of the preacher's fear of causing offence. This may be more of a problem for women preachers than for men.

EXPECTANCY

Effective preaching will only happen where there is a sense of expectancy, on the part of both the congregation and the preacher.

There is still a sense of expectancy as the preacher mounts the pulpit. Admittedly, that expectancy can be lost very quickly. As is often noted, we belong to an episodic culture which encourages us to flit from experience to experience, to 'channel surf' rather than give sustained attention. Most preachers realize how important it is not to allow their listeners to switch off during those crucial first few minutes. However, this expectancy has little to do with the wish to be entertained or diverted for the next fifteen minutes. It has to do with the expectancy of the listeners for encounter with the Living Word in nurture, challenge or comfort.

The expectancy of the listeners will be influenced by (though thankfully not totally dependent on) the expectancy of the preacher for transformation and change (conversion). Preachers will be expectant insofar as they are willing to take risks and to make themselves vulnerable (open to the Spirit) in terms of content and style. The well-prepared full script can easily become, in the pulpit, the well-protected safe sermon instead of the risky one-off 'breaking of the word' which surprises and transforms both congregation and preacher.

The sermon may begin studiously and conscientiously in the study; it may be successfully presented in the pulpit; but the word of God will only be 'broken' and 'taken' as preacher and congregation listen expectantly to one another.

PREACHING AND PERSONALITY

Angela Butler

The most powerful influence on our communication will be our personality. The Myers-Briggs Personality Type Indicator (MBTI®) gives some helpful insights which can make us aware of our own personality biases and so can help us to maximize our effectiveness. Further, in all communication it is important to take account not just of our own personality preferences but those of our hearers.

Since preaching is primarily about the way in which we impart information and insights and others receive it, I start with a look at typical ways which, according to the MBTI®, people impart or collect information using their 'Perceiving' functions—their preference for either **Sensing** or **iNtuition**.

Are you, or have you heard, the preacher with a preference for Sensing whose gift is to be concrete and practical? These are the folk who prefer facts and like to live in the real world. They like a sequential, detailed presentation which, in focusing on the details, may ignore or miss the big picture. They are also likely to focus on the present and the past as opposed to the future and to be literal in their use of words. They are likely to have a down-to-earth spirituality which is looking for a practical application of the Scriptures and so may be able to help people by systematic explanations of issues. However, iNtuitive types may quickly tire of Sensers' presentations because of the detail, and accuse them of being dull and failing to see the wood for the trees.

Or perhaps you are, or have heard, the preacher with a preference for iNtuition whose gift is vision, which enables them to see the big picture, the wider perspective. They are sometimes mystics who may prefer theory and abstraction, inspiration and insight, to facts and details. Because iNtuitives tend to have leap-frog minds they are able to make connections and identify patterns through a variety of media. Symbols can be important to them and be full of suggestions. They may be able to help people with thoughts and ideas that come 'out of the blue'. But Sensing types may lose the iNtuitives' thread and accuse them of having their heads in the clouds and their feet off the ground.

When it comes to making decisions on what we have heard using our Sensing or iNtuition, other parts of personality, called the 'Judging' functions, come into play—**Thinking** or **Feeling**.

Are you, or have you heard, the preacher with a preference for Thinking whose gift is logical analysis and the ability to see things objectively? This person enables us to take a long view or to spot inconsistencies or evasions in an argument. They may instinctively find themselves homing in on questions about what is true or just and may emphasize justice above mercy. They may like using words such as 'principles', 'policy', 'firmness', 'justice', 'standards', 'analysis' and 'strategy' and they often make excellent expositors. They tend to be convincing and make decisions based on what is logically true. However, Feeling types hearing them may tire of the emphasis on theological abstraction and accuse them of missing the very heart of the gospel which cries out for compassion, understanding and human warmth.

Or perhaps you are, or have heard, the Feeling preacher whose gift is the ability to see things from within a situation. This person enables us to empathize with, or see things from, other people's viewpoint and to consider their thoughts and feelings. They are primarily concerned about relationships and harmony. As a result their preaching may some-times either fail to challenge or appear to be passionate. Their favourite words may include 'love', 'mercy', 'humane', 'harmony', 'good or bad', 'sympathy' or 'devotion'. They tend to make decisions using personal convictions based on moral or ethical values; so Feeling people are likely to be interested in other people's values and where they come from. However, the Thinking types hearing them may quickly become impati-ent with this emphasis on interpersonal matters and accuse them of failing to grasp the hard intellectual issues and the pressing challenges and contradictions of the faith.

The other aspects of personality—**Extraversion** and **Introversion**, **Judgment** and **Perception**—will also have an impact on the way in which we preach, but may be less evident from the pulpit. For instance, when we are speaking we have to use Extraversion, whether or not it is our natural preference—the main thing we may have to guard against as extraverts might be to become too long-winded as new ideas or thoughts come to mind.

Judgment is the gift of order and structure which enables us to plan in advance and organize. People who prefer to use a Judgment process to run their outer world tend to want to give conclusive evidence on which people can make decisions. They are likely therefore to draw sermons to a clear conclusion on which people can make a decision. On the other hand, if we prefer Judgment we may preach a message which seems demanding, rigid or restrictive to others. The Perceptive types hearing us may quickly become uncomfortable with this approach and may fidget or inwardly rebel in an attempt to keep an issue open for debate as long as possible. If too planned or inflexible, our efforts may not take into account the unforeseen.

Perception is the gift of being able to go with the flow. People who prefer to use a Perception process to run their outer world enjoy exploring and processing things. For them the journey is probably more important than the arrival so they may express inquisitiveness and want to keep the issue open for as long as possible in case any new information comes to light which might affect their decision. They are therefore wonderfully flexible and adaptable to situations or circumstances. But if we prefer Perception we may preach a message which is so exploratory or adaptable that we become long-winded, side-tracked or inconclusive. The Judging types hearing us may get impatient with our lack of structure or organization of material and write us off as wishy-washy or unsure of our ground.

If there are so many personality factors to consider in preaching, how can we possibly cater for everyone? One of the simplest frameworks which is said to cater for the four functions is to include in sermons (or services) all of the following:

- For those with a preference for **Sensing**—something concrete and practical
- For those with a preference for **iNtuition**—something of vision
- For those with a preference for **Thinking**—some understanding
- For those with a preference for **Feeling**—silence

The latter is, of course, the one which is most neglected in our preaching and worship today, but I wonder how many preachers can testify to how much more powerful has been the three to five minutes' silence (or carefully chosen, quiet, non-congregational music) after their sermons than five minutes' more of spoken word? Maybe that's the opportunity we are missing—giving God his turn to have the last word!

PREACHING AND GENDER

Jane Craske

Gender is one of the defining factors in who we are as human beings and, therefore, who we are, created male and female, before God. So, given the above heading, don't automatically read 'for women preachers only'!

Christian preaching in the 21st century takes place in a tradition that is gendered. Until relatively recently, almost all preaching was done by men. (The one consistent exception over centuries, allowing women to speak in public, was the Quaker tradition.) Does that history matter? Even today, most preaching is still undertaken by men. Preachers who are men are the 'norm', as analysed by gender, and preachers who are women are not. Men and women who preach are quite simply in different places when it comes to where their preaching is sited in the Christian tradition. Some women, *even in traditions that have welcomed women as preachers for many years*, feel before them a barrier not just of uncertainty about fitness or ability but a question about whether they should or should not preach *because of their gender*.

How should Christian communities today understand and use biblical passages that enshrine gendered restrictions? It is, after all, the business of the preacher to interpret Scripture for today's Christian community. Therefore we are the ones to ask questions about the extent to which biblical passages reflect their social context, and whether that social context is the same thing as God's purposes for women and men today.

Implicit in the vocation of preaching is an obligation to be aware of our selves in social context, interpreted in theological perspective. I am one of the people God has called to proclaim the gospel in the particular form of public preaching, and that 'I' matters to my preaching. I am not simply an empty vessel, or just a microphone for God. God instead takes the risk of using my personality, my commitments and even my mistakes in the model that incarnation gives us of how God works.

Part of the formation of any preacher is the formation of a gendered person. We may at present be more or less conscious of ourselves as gendered, or of how the formation of that aspect of our humanity took place. We are also formed by class background, by ethnicity, by our sexuality or by our abilities, let alone by the events that have shaped and changed us. But I believe we become better persons and better preachers as we become more conscious of ourselves, because we can thereby become more conscious of who we are in relation to God.

We need to recognize gender stereotyping, cultural restrictions on women or on men, when we collude with them, when we uphold them and when we challenge them. Such things may have theological groundings for us, and theological repercussions which will appear in our preaching. What do you believe about God's creation of men and women as equal, or different, or both, and what might that imply about God? Are you aware of how differently others believe and why? To what extent are you continuing to examine and seek further clarity in those beliefs and the practices that flow from them? We need to gain critical distance, in order not simply to peddle our own prejudices or the assumptions we grew up with as Christian truth for all times and all circumstances. We need to understand these factors for the sake of better understanding and preaching about how God works in the world and how God transforms the human person.

Does the gender of the preacher matter? In Christian churches we will still find every response between 'not at all' and 'of course, obviously!' Those who preach need to allow gender its weight as they understand the world and themselves before God, but they ought not to allow gender to enforce restrictive distinctions between men and women and therefore between individuals who all have their varied gifts and patterns of response to God's grace.

✿

CRITERIA FOR EVALUATING PREACHING

John James (1983)

What is it that goes to make a good sermon? The answer is by no means simple. We can approach it on different levels.

We may examine the *technique*. Did it have a good opening, a sound underlying structure and an appropriate conclusion? Was there a clear aim? Or was it the 'Jericho' type of sermon in which the preacher goes all round the subject seven times, making a lot of noise, convinced that the walls of the listeners' resistance must finally fall?

We can also have a look at *theological content*. Was it really a Christian sermon? Did it offer the congregation any fresh resources? Or merely quench the smoking flax? Paul Harms speaks of an address given at a Lenten midweek service to the 'faithful of the faithful': 'One would think that every Judas, every Pilate, every Herod, and every Caiaphas of every generation had wandered into that house of worship, there to receive the tongue-lashing of their lives administered with the consummate skill of a man who has dedicated his life to the Sinaitic codes.'

Or we may think about the *delivery*. Was it audible? Were the pace and voice-range varied appropriately? What use did the preacher make of hands and eyes? Were there any distracting mannerisms?

These are some of the elementary things that one can look for, but from the human sciences and from modern communication studies other important criteria have emerged—factors neglected or often entirely ignored in the pulpit oratory of the past. Here we are thinking less of what is happening in the pulpit and more of what (if anything) is going on in the pew.

Was there, for instance, any real *relationship*? Did the congregation feel that the preacher understood and accepted them—their problems and point of view? Or did he or she 'pontificate'? Were they content merely to utter a series of statements from on high?

Any lack of feeling or goodwill between two people will tend to distort or even block all communication between them. It may well determine whether an otherwise excellent sermon misses or goes home.

Empathy will always encourage an attitude of *respect for the listener*. One of the hallmarks of Jesus' teaching was his readiness to allow people to come to see the truth in their own way and in their own time (for example, Mark 10:17–22; John 6:60–71).

Did the congregation feel that the preacher was seeking to impose his or her own views upon them with a 'take it or leave it' attitude? Did he or she respect their right to be what they are and to grow freely in insight and understanding? Or were they left with the impression that he or she was using divine or biblical authority rather to bolster their own uncertainty?

Much will depend, in other words, upon the preacher's own credibility and trustworthiness. What matters here is *authenticity or genuineness*. Did the preacher seem to be hiding behind an impersonal mask, a third-person approach like the royal use of the pronoun 'one'? Or was he or she present in person—natural, human and relaxed?

In Richard Strauss's opera *Capriccio* there is a fascinating discussion between the poet and the musician, Olivier and Flamand, as to which should come first—the words or the music. They finally decide that in the ideal performance both must go together as brother and sister. In the ideal sermon the message and the messenger are at one.

Authenticity will naturally express itself in an appropriate style and language—appropriate, that is, both to the speaker and to the occasion. It will be concrete, natural and direct rather than the language of an essay.

One of the qualities lacking in many a sermon can best be described as *nowness*. Sometimes we never seem to leave Palestine or the past. We may even be left with the impression that we can never really mature in the Christian faith without a detailed knowledge of the antiquities of the Greco-Roman world or the Hebrew text of the Psalms.

Any message with impact must also have a sense of immediacy and relevance. Paul reminded his Corinthian readers that 'now is the accepted time', 'now is the day of salvation'. Yet as Clyde Fant comments, 'I do not enjoy many advantages over the apostle Paul, but there is one unique advantage which is mine: I am here and he is not.'

An important key to relevance is suggested by the Greek word *skandalon* (stumbling-block). The message of the gospel not only has an immediacy about it but also a certain 'cutting edge'. The cross must challenge before it can save and often hurt before it can heal. Did the sermon leave us largely unaffected and unmoved? Or was there a sense of freshness and urgency about it? Were we 'cut to the quick'?

The danger here, of course, is that the preacher may seem to be setting himself or herself apart or even posing as an exception. That is one reason why preaching must always include some element of personal testimony. Credibility requires that somehow the preacher, too, must be seen to be living under the same searching scrutiny—a recipient of the same all-sufficient grace. Some *self-disclosure* there must be, but too much too soon will be as bad as too little too late. The adjective 'appropriate' is all-important.

The vital question is: did you really learn anything about the preacher herself that helped or encouraged you? And the converse equally matters: was there anything that only emphasized the distance between you or that put you off?

The model for all New Testament communication is 'the Word made flesh'. In the end God's Word is made known to others through our own full and true humanity—not by the suppression of it. It is a strength that is made perfect through weakness.

❦

KEEPING ON TARGET

Gethin Thomas

Success in preaching can be the great enemy of progress. Good preaching can be the enemy of better preaching. Contentment with the way preaching is can limit our view of how much better it could become. We are accountable to God and his people to offer the highest and best in our preaching. The old adage says, 'Never be satisfied with your preaching: once you are, nobody else will be.'

It has been said that preaching without feedback is like driving golf balls in the dark. Unless we hear from our hearers, we never know if we are hitting the turf or going off into the green. Feedback ensures that we have satisfactorily done what we were called to do and helps us to do even better in our preaching.

Bill Hybels deals with the subject of feedback and evaluation in the book *Mastering Contemporary Preaching* (IVP, with Stuart Briscoe and Haddon Robinson). In the chapter entitled 'Keeping Ourselves on Target', Hybels remarks that every preacher is evaluated, one way or another, by every listener. Constructive evaluation won't happen, though, no matter how willing we are to receive it, unless we are asking the right people the right questions at the right time.

THE RIGHT PEOPLE

Preaching is a two-way street, involving the preacher and the listener. We need to acknowledge and listen to those who listen to us. There are many people who comment on our preaching, whether we like it or not. People will always evaluate our preaching in casual conversation, perhaps after the service has ended, or around the meal table at home. We might be surprised what helpful feedback these casual conversations could yield.

We should also bear in mind people who could be specifically asked to comment on our preaching. Often there is no better critic or consumer of our sermons than our spouse. It may be that we will look for a preaching partner. This person, as well as listening to us as we preach, may look at video recordings or listen to cassette recordings of our sermons with us and offer good, reflective and honest comments. Preaching workshops could be attended that have a specific sermon feedback session. People who can be honest without worrying about harming us are very important in this process.

There could be selected, designated feedback from a chosen group who will be specifically asked to listen and respond critically to our sermons. If we use an official feedback group, we should be careful not to create a group who are listening so critically that they are detached from the worship. Be aware that such critics, particularly if we listen to them and follow their advice, could turn out to be our biggest fans. It would be wise to change the selected group every three months. Make sure the feedback is representative of people as a whole within the congregation, not just a handful of the extremely vocal. We can learn from this kind of critic but sometimes they do not truly represent the congregation as a whole.

We'll certainly get responses from people who care about us. We should take what they say to heart because often it comes from the heart. They want us to become more effective and dynamic preachers so that they can be helped towards becoming more effective and dynamic Christians. We can use such feedback as a basis for learning new things and trying new approaches. Obtaining individuals' views on preaching helps us and the congregation in our task of being a good learning community.

THE RIGHT QUESTIONS

To stay right on target, as well as asking the right people, we need to be asking the right questions. This becomes part of a conscious effort to gain feedback rather than relying on random and casual comments. There can be written as well as spoken responses. Regular sermon feedback sheets or the occasional use of a preaching questionnaire can put specific questions about people's reactions, with opportunity to make suggestions about future sermons. Such questions might include:

- What did you appreciate about this sermon?
- What distracted you in this sermon?
- What suggestions can you offer me for better practice?

In asking people for specific and structured feedback we often learn much about our style of preaching, and we learn what the congregation actually heard rather than what we thought they might be hearing. The right questions will not encourage a negative and destructive response that focuses on fault-finding and which can leave the preacher feeling condemned and belittled; they will elicit critique rather than criticism. They can encourage a response to our preaching that is positive, constructive and focuses on the whole person, including their strengths as well as their weaknesses. They will enable praise and encouragement, calling for celebration as well as pointing to areas for correction. Often preachers are harder on their preaching than their listeners are. Encouragement and affirmation are often the outcome of the right questions asked by the preacher to the right people about the preaching, assisting the growth of confidence and creativity.

THE RIGHT TIME

To stay right on target, we need also to be asking for feedback *at the right time*. Some will say that feedback can be gained as a sermon is being preached. Observing the congregations' responses does not give me specific information about *how* my sermon is being heard, but it does tell me *whether or not* I am being listened to.

Often feedback immediately after the service in which the sermon has been preached will indicate how helpful my sermon has been to my listeners. Eye contact and the warm handshakes after the sermon will often reveal as much about my sermon as anything that has been said verbally or written down. The ongoing pastoral conversations in the following weeks and months will often tell much about the worth and value of my preaching to those who listen. Sometimes it is easier to give and receive responses to the sermon after there has been time for thoughtful reflection. Some preachers leave feedback cards or forms in the seats for people to fill in straight after a sermon. These can be left every Sunday for comment. Writing comments to be collected in and read by the preacher later will often allow for anonymous feedback and it frees people to be more honest. This method might allow for another person trusted by the preacher to gather up the written feedback and present it to the preacher in its most helpful form.

Such feedback does not have to be offered after every single sermon. Some preachers would have an occasional group of sermons assessed in this way. Other experienced preachers would caution against paying serious attention to listeners' comments, particularly at times when the preacher is feeling low, vulnerable or disillusioned. This would certainly not be the right time for asking for critical feedback; on the other hand, positive, affirming responses at these times could be very beneficial.

RIGHT ON TARGET

Preachers need to find the people, questions and times that will be best for them. These right people, questions and times may change as circumstances change. But all feedback that encourages reflection, experimentation, creativity and variety on the preacher's part is to be welcomed, and can keep us right on target.

FURTHER READING

Martyn D. Atkins, *Preaching in a Cultural Context*, Foundery Press, 2001.

Richard Bewes, *Speaking in Public—Effectively*, Christian Focus Publications, 1998.

R.E.C. Browne, *The Ministry of the Word*, SCM Press, 1958/1976.

Walter Brueggemann, *Cadences of Home: Preaching among Exiles*, Westminster John Knox Press, 1997.

Donald Coggan, *A New Day for Preaching: the Sacrament of the Word*, SPCK, 1996.

Fred B. Craddock, *Preaching*, Abingdon Press, 1985.

Jane V. Craske, *A Woman's Perspective on Preaching*, Foundery Press, 2001.

David Day, *A Preaching Workbook*, Lynx, 1998.

Richard L. Eslinger, *The Web of Preaching: New Options in Homiletic Method*, Abingdon Press, 2002.

Sidney Greidanus, *The Modern Preacher and the Ancient Text*, Eerdmans, 1988.

Thomas Long, *The Witness of Preaching*, Westminster John Knox Press, 1989.

Eugene L. Lowry, *The Homiletical Plot: the Sermon as Narrative Art Form*, expanded ed., Westminster John Knox Press, 2001.

Henry H. Mitchell, *Black Preaching: the Recovery of a Powerful Art*, Abingdon Press, 1991.

Jolyon P. Mitchell, *Visually Speaking: Radio and the Renaissance of Preaching*, T. & T. Clark, 1999.

Colin Morris, *Raising the Dead: the Art of the Preacher as Public Performer*, Fount, 1996.

Sue Page, *Away with Words*, Lynx, 1998.

Christine Pilkington, *Preaching on the Old Testament*, Foundery Press, 2000.

Michael Quicke, *360-Degree Preaching*, Baker/Paternoster, 2003.

David J. Schlafer, *Surviving the Sermon: a Guide to Preaching for Those who Have to Listen*, Cowley Publications, 1992.

David J. Schlafer, *What Makes this Day Different? Preaching Grace on Special Occasions*, Cowley Publications, 1998.

The following booklets published by Grove deal usefully and briefly with aspects of preaching.

B4: Bob Fyall, *Preaching Old Testament Narrative*, 1997.

B20: Stephen Wright, *Preaching with the Grain of Scripture*, 2001.

Ev25: Chris Edmondson, *How Shall They Hear? Preaching Evangelistically*, 1994.

Ev47: Angela Butler, *Personality and Communicating the Gospel*, 1999.

Ev58: Roger Standing, *Preaching for the Unchurched*, 2002.

P68: Jeremy Thompson, *Preaching as Dialogue: Is the Sermon a Sacred Cow?*, 1996.

P86: Nick Watson, *Sorrow and Hope: Preaching at Funerals*, 2001.

W139: John Leach, *Responding to Preaching*, 1997/2001.

W144: Tim Stratford, *Interactive Preaching: Opening the Word then Listening*, 1998.

W164: Charles Chadwick and Philip Tovey, *Developing Reflective Practice for Preachers*, 2001.

For more information on resources and events offered by the College of Preachers, contact the Administrator, 14A North Street, Bourne, Lincolnshire PE10 9AB.
Tel/Fax: 01778 422929; E-mail administrator@collegeofpreachers.org.uk
Website: www.collegeofpreachers.org.uk

Guidelines is a unique Bible reading resource that offers four months of in-depth study written by leading scholars. Contributors are drawn from around the world, as well as the UK, and represent a stimulating and thought-provoking breadth of Christian tradition.

Instead of the usual dated daily readings, *Guidelines* provides weekly units, broken into at least six sections, plus an introduction giving context for the passage, and a final section of points for thought and prayer. On any day you can read as many or as few sections as you wish, to fit in with work or home routine. As well as a copy of *Guidelines*, you will need a Bible. Each contributor also suggests books for further study.

Guidelines is edited by Dr Katharine Dell, Senior Lecturer in the Faculty of Divinity at Cambridge University and Director of Studies in Theology at St Catharine's College, and Dr Jeremy Duff, Tutor in New Testament at Wycliffe Hall and a member of the Theology Faculty of Oxfor University.

GUIDELINES SUBSCRIPTIONS

❏ I would like to give a gift subscription
(please complete both name and address sections below)
❏ I would like to take out a subscription myself
(complete name and address details only once)

This completed coupon should be sent with appropriate payment to BRF. Alternatively, please write to us quoting your name, address, the subscription you would like for either yourself or a friend (with their name and address), the start date and credit card number, expiry date and signature if paying by credit card.

Gift subscription name _____

Gift subscription address _____

_____ Postcode _____

Please send to the above, beginning with the next January/May/September* issue.
(* *delete as applicable)*

(please tick box)	UK	SURFACE	AIR MAIL
GUIDELINES	❏ £11.40	❏ £12.75	❏ £15.00
GUIDELINES 3-year sub	❏ £28.95		

Please complete the payment details below and send your coupon, with appropriate payment to: **BRF, First Floor, Elsfield Hall, 15–17 Elsfield Way, Oxford OX2 8FG**

Your name _____

Your address _____

_____ Postcode _____

Total enclosed £ _____ (cheques should be made payable to 'BRF')

Payment by cheque ❏ postal order ❏ Visa ❏ Mastercard ❏ Switch ❏

Card number: ☐☐☐☐ ☐☐☐☐ ☐☐☐☐ ☐☐☐☐

Expiry date of card: ☐☐☐☐ Issue number (Switch): ☐☐☐☐

Signature (essential if paying by credit/Switch card) _____

NB: BRF notes are also available from your local Christian bookshop.   **BRF is a Registered Charity**

THE MINISTRY OF THE WORD

A HANDBOOK FOR PREACHERS
ON THE COMMON WORSHIP LECTIONARY

EDITED BY NAOMI STARKEY

An essential companion for all preachers and teachers, *The Ministry of the Word* brings together a distinguished team of contributors to write helpful comments on the core of the Common Worship Lectionary—the Bible readings set for the main weekly Sunday services as well as for the festival highlights of the Church's year. The concise reflections bring out the focus and particular emphasis of each passage, and will help anyone who has to prepare sermons, talks and studies for congregations and smaller groups alike.

The contributors are:
  The Revd Dr Robert Fyall
  The Revd Dr Alan Garrow
  The Revd Dr Michael Gilbertson
  Mrs Margaret Killingray
  The Rev Dr Ian Paul
  The Revd John Proctor
  Dr Deborah Rooke
  Prebendary Gill Sumner
  Dom Henry Wansbrough

ISBN 1 84101 117 7   £20.00
To order, please turn to page 175

THE RITE STUFF

RITUAL IN CONTEMPORARY CHRISTIAN WORSHIP AND MISSION

EDITED BY PETE WARD

Ritual is having something of a revival in church, as some Christians start to explore ways of prayer and worship from more ancient traditions. In the past ritual has sometimes been derided as 'empty', but in fact it focuses meaning. It can help our worship be ecstatic but also rooted in daily life. It can help us express our feelings for fellow believers and at the same time lift us into the presence of our God.

In this book, each chapter explores a different aspect of ritual and faith. The range of these discussions is quite wide, but the unifying factor is the growing appreciation of the significance of ritual for worship and spirituality in postmodernity.

The contributors are:
 Jonny Baker
 Maggi Dawn
 Ana Draper
 Jeremy Fletcher
 Anthony Reddie
 Mike Riddell
 Pete Ward

ISBN 1 84101 227 0   £8.99
Published May 2004
To order, please turn to page 175

JACOB AND THE PRODIGAL

HOW JESUS RETOLD ISRAEL'S STORY

KENNETH E. BAILEY

Israel, the community to which Jesus belonged, took its name from the patriarch Jacob. His story of exile and return was Israel's story as well. This book examines the well-known parable of the prodigal son and shows how, in telling it, Jesus took the story of Jacob and reshaped it in his own way and for his own purposes.

The comparative study of the Old Testament family saga and the New Testament parable unpacks the similarities and the differences between the two texts. Why did Jesus make the changes in the story that he did? What was he seeking to say about himself and about the people he called his own?

In writing *Jacob and the Prodigal*, Kenneth Bailey draws on a lifetime of study in Middle Eastern culture, the Gospels and, in particular, the parable of the prodigal son. In the process, he offers a fresh view of how Jesus interpreted Israel's past, his present and their future.

ISBN 1 84101 358 7   £12.99
To order, please turn to page 175

THE STORY WE LIVE BY

A READER'S GUIDE TO THE NEW TESTAMENT

R. ALASTAIR CAMPBELL

At the heart of Christianity is a story—not a code nor a creed, but the story of Jesus. Christians have lived by this story for centuries and return to it again and again to renew faith and deepen understanding. This book is an accessible introduction to how that story is presented in the New Testament, firstly in the four different accounts of Jesus' life, death and resurrection, followed by the early years of the Church and the ensuing series of letters and commentaries on those events.

Starting with an analysis of the four Gospels, *The Story We Live By* shows how the New Testament writers shaped their material to communicate the truth of Jesus' teaching to their audiences and how their writings arise from and still maintain continuity with the Old Testament. It also covers issues such as authorship, textual dating and the different literary forms used from sermons to apocalypse.

ISBN 1 84101 359 5   £12.99
To order, please turn to page 175

ORDER FORM

REF	TITLE	PRICE	QTY	TOTAL
117 7	*The Ministry of the Word*	£20.00		
227 0	*The Rite Stuff*	£8.99		
358 7	*Jacob and the Prodigal*	£12.99		
359 5	*The Story We Live By*	£12.99		

POSTAGE AND PACKING CHARGES					Postage and packing:	
order value	UK	Europe	Surface	Air Mail	Donation:	
£7.00 & under	£1.25	£3.00	£3.50	£5.50	**Total enclosed:**	
£7.01–£30.00	£2.25	£5.50	£6.50	£10.00		
Over £30.00	free	prices on request				

Name _____ Account Number _____

Address_____

_____ Postcode _____

Telephone Number _____ Email _____

Payment by: Cheque ❏ Mastercard ❏ Visa ❏ Postal Order ❏ Switch ❏

Credit card no. ❏❏❏❏ ❏❏❏❏ ❏❏❏❏ ❏❏❏❏   Expires ❏❏ ❏❏

Switch card no. ❏❏❏❏❏❏❏❏❏❏❏❏❏❏❏❏❏❏

Issue no. of Switch card ❏❏❏❏   Expires ❏❏ ❏❏

Signature _____ Date _____

All orders must be accompanied by the appropriate payment.

Please send your completed order form to:
BRF, First Floor, Elsfield Hall, 15–17 Elsfield Way, Oxford OX2 8FG
Tel. 01865 319700 / Fax. 01865 319701 Email: enquiries@brf.org.uk

❏ Please send me further information about BRF publications.

Available from your local Christian bookshop.   BRF is a Registered Charity

brf

Resourcing your spiritual journey

through...

- Bible reading notes
- Books for Advent & Lent
- Books for Bible study and prayer
- Books to resource those working with
  under 11s in school, church and at home

- Quiet days and retreats
- Training for primary teachers
  and children's leaders
- Godly Play
- Barnabas Live

For more information, visit the **brf** website at **www.brf.org.uk**